21 Days

For the Excelling Soul

Daily devotional to walk in your God given purpose and to enhance your relationship with Christ.

May All the
dreams God hAS
given you in
the SupernAturAl
come to pASS in the
nAturAl 'th HASte !!

Blessings /

21 Days

For the Excelling Soul

Daily devotional to walk in your God given purpose and to enhance your relationship with Christ.

Blessing JK Monday

HE IS DIVINE
— PUBLICATIONS, LLC —

21 Days for the Excelling Soul

Copyright © 2020 by Blessing JK Monday

All scriptures are taken from the King James Version of the Holy Bible unless otherwise noted.

Printed in the United States of America
First Printing, 2020
ISBN 978-1-7357362-0-4

Published by:
He Is Divine Publications, LLC
heisdivinepub@gmail.com

Cover & Interior Design: Wendi Hayman, Glory to Glory Publications, LLC
www.wendihayman.com | glorytoglorypublications@gmail.com

Table of Contents

Dedication

This book is dedicated to all these wonderful people in my life: Roland Gonletuo, Agnes Gonletuo, Waripere Nelson, Prince-Michael Wehye, Love-Eden Sudue, Jeanette Doe, Christian and Britney Sudue, Syera Weah, Farlor Gono, Michael Willor, Jason Weah, Prince Amiekumo, Charleston Matalda, Joshua Porte, Christ Maouene, Kate Matike and Albertine Cooper.

Acknowledgments

Special thanks to my husband, Uchechukwu Monday, who God brought into my life at just the right time. You shower me with true, unconditional love. You are my motivator, my extra source of strength and my number one best friend. You have me for life. Thank you for all your love and encouragement to keep this work going. You are one of God's greatest gifts to me.

Big thanks to Chekanaeh Glory Ministries International for sponsoring this book. Thank you for your generous funding in making this book possible! Thank you for your major contribution to spreading the gospel for 10+ years. I am so grateful.

Thank you, Minister Jesus Christ Princess (mommy), for always reminding me to complete this book. Thank you for being bold for the gospel in action and truth. Thank you for building my siblings and me in the Word of God. You are my biggest role model, and I will forever look up to you.

To my partner in prayer (P.I.P.) Olivia Akinpelu, thank you for being a great sister. Thank you for the prayers, the love, and the laughs, especially during the darkest of times. You are a jewel to be cherished and forever in my heart.

To my mother-in-law, Evangelist Amaefule Ijeoma Edith, thank you for working endlessly in the vineyard of the Lord. Thank you for praying endlessly for our family. Thank you for being a great mother and a spiritual backbone for us all.

Bernice Morris, my first lady and friend. Thank you for all your encouragement, prayers, love and support. Thank you for loving on me and fasting with me. I enjoy all our dinner dates in which we can commune about the Lord and life. I cherish you and all your wisdom.

Tressa Smallwood, thank you for being a great mentor and leader. Thank you for always showing me patience. God led me to you for this exact purpose. You are knowledgeable in what you do and such a great help. I am grateful that we crossed paths.

The best for last: Thank you, Daddy Jesus, my Lord and Savior. The Lord of my life that I will serve forever. Lord, I am forever indebted to you. Thank you for always believing in me, even when I don't believe in myself. I love you, Lord.

Introduction

During these times, many are in a place of confusion about their purpose and who they are. Sadly, these same issues also plague our brothers and sisters in the body of Christ. Some even question how they can make it in this world without selling out on their faith. This truth-inspired devotional is for whoever is struggling with these thoughts. This devotional will give you the extra strength and reassurance you need to get through and refocus.

This daily devotional highlights often overlooked keys in our walk with God that He has used to help me. So, in obedience, I am now sharing with you. True success in this world comes from knowing your God-given purpose and walking through obedience in God's commandments. Whatever God has called you to do, walking in His will allows you to have the fulfilling life that you've longed for. True success comes from having a deep relationship with the Father and receiving only His incorruptible blessings (James 5:2; Matthew 6:19).

This book is NOT, however, for anyone who just wants to come to Christ to receive His riches and glory without having a true relationship with Him in obedience. If this is the motive, you are only deceiving yourself (James 4:3; Deuteronomy 8:18).

While reading this daily devotional, I challenge you to be

an active reader and really soak up this material and the word of God. Read the scripture citations in the text, take notes, think about how the material correlates to your life and what the Lord is saying to you. I will encourage you to fast while reading this devotional (yes, for 21 days)! It may not be the whole day; it may just be taking an hour or two before the Lord each day to focus only on Him. Step away from social media and distractions during your quiet time with God. Digest everything that is in this book for your own benefit. How far are you willing to go to know your Creator and what you are meant to do in this life? Beloved, you are special, unique and one of a kind. You cannot successfully complete anyone's life but your own.

So take this devotional very seriously! Get excited about what the Lord is going to reveal to you in these 21 days! Keep this book as a reference when you need to be refreshed! Share this good news with someone and be a light to anyone who is lost the same way you were!

Regarding receiving your God-given purpose, your strengthened relationship with Christ, and your new success with Him, I stand in agreement with you (Matthew 18:19).

Father, in the name of Jesus, I pray that You touch and open the hearts of anyone who reads this devotional. I decree and declare a new awakening in their spirits. Holy Spirit, become active in their lives. Let them take these lessons seriously. Let their calling be revealed unto them and give them the strength to follow through. Give them new confidence that is from You. Increase their faith and give them an extra measure of grace. Wipe away the cloud of confusion that is above them. Lead them through these 21 days and let there be a spiritual and visible change in their lives, Lord! With haste! As Your word says in Revelation, let there be testimonies that follow. We thank You for everything, Lord Jesus. We seal this prayer in the mighty name of Jesus. Amen.

Dream On, Joseph

"And afterward, I will pour out my Spirit on all people. Your sons and daughters will prophesy, your old men will dream dreams, your young men will see visions." Joel 2:28

Today's Scripture Reading:
Job 33:14-18; Genesis 37:5-11; Genesis 41:25-27; Genesis 41:37-44 and Matthew 1:20-23

I always marvel at the beauty of flowers. They're so many, so diverse. Their attractive colors draw your attention to their distinctive structures. Each one is so different and serves a different purpose. Each one blesses the world with its particular purpose. It is even more amazing that they are formed by something so simple as a seed. It is unimaginable that something so small can later blossom into something so beautiful. This is the same idea that you should have toward your dreams.

Like any blossoming flower, a dream originates as a seed; it is planted, grown, and later harvested for a particular purpose. Your dream should be protected. It should be greatly guarded because it is the beginning of life to your destiny. It births a purpose greater than you could ever imagine. Like the seed of a flower, how you nurture and care for your dream will determine its outcome. If it is grown poorly, it could die; however, it will flourish if it is well taken care of.

Throughout the Bible, the Lord used dreams and visions to speak to His people. He used them to forewarn people of imminent danger or inform them of the bountiful promises coming their way. This was the case for Joseph. Through a dream, God revealed to him that he would be a great man, and because of how powerful his dreams were, his brothers became extremely angry and jealous (Genesis 37:10-11). In the end, Joseph became just what he had dreamed, and his dreams became a reality. His dreams depicted what was going to happen in the future! He practically became a pharaoh that helped the nation and his family through a time of famine. His family had to humbly bow and come to him to seek food, just as his dreams showed years prior (Genesis 42:6). Another example is when an angel of the Lord appeared to Joseph, Jesus's earthly father, to inform him that his bride-to-be would conceive the Savior of the world (Matthew 1:20-23). Dreams are linked to the spiritual realm, and most often, if you dreamt it, it has already come to pass in the supernatural, which will later manifest in the natural realm.

I have had many dreams and visions. The Lord would often reveal to me who was trying to hurt me, the type of people I should stay away from, and even new, creative ideas. Every dream that I have had has become a reality. I never take them for granted or brush them off, and you shouldn't either! They are direct messages from the Holy Spirit that reveal what is going on in ways that your physical eyes cannot see.

Dreams are very crucial to your success because they are the first phase of anything you do in life. It is also important to guard your heart because everything flows from it. Even your dreams can become influenced by your thoughts (Proverbs 4:23). Owning a business, making a major decision, having a child, naming a child, deciding where to move, creating ideas or making major plans all come from the thoughts you envisioned. For that reason, you don't want your visions to become foggy by polluting them with unnecessary dark content. Philippians 4:8 (KJV) tells us, "Whatsoever things are true, whatsoever things are honest, whatsoever things are just, whatsoever things are pure, whatsoever things are of good report; if there be any virtue, and if there be any praise, think on these things."

Meditating on godly thoughts and imaginations will have a ripple effect on your visions and dreams because you are not clouding your spirit with sinful and dark thinking. The Lord will have the opportunity to infiltrate your mind with thoughts from Him, therefore creating a clear godly flow of communication from Him to you.

Maybe you have been receiving dreams for an extensive period of time now. Maybe you have neglected your dreams because you think you can never amount to them or because you've failed in the past trying to reach them. Maybe you do not spend enough time with the Lord to hear from Him. He's talking, but you're not hearing Him. Or it could be that you just don't understand these dreams. The Lord is the only one who can truly reveal to you the meaning of your dreams (Genesis 40:8). Open your heart to Him and seek understanding.

If you haven't been dreaming, ask the Lord to give you dreams. Ask the Lord to give you visions as well. Ask the Lord to reveal vital information to you when you sleep at night. God reveals in so many ways what you are destined to be. He longs to speak with you. Since I've asked the Lord to give me dreams and help me remember my dreams, I have been experiencing so many! This is the time when the Lord is freely giving out dreams and visions (Joel 2:28; Acts 2:17).

Aside from asking God to help you recall your dreams, try to remember to protect your visions and dreams at all costs. Don't be in a hurry to explain to everyone what your special dreams are. Don't give the enemy an open door to come in and destroy what you may not even fully understand yet. If others find out about your dreams and mock you, pay no attention to them. Joseph was mocked too (Genesis 37:5-8)! Not everybody is meant to understand what the Father has fully designed for YOU alone. They can't understand because it doesn't belong to them.

So, dreamer, what dreams have you been having? What visions have you been having? What are those images that spark your mind and interrupt your train of thought? What has been plaguing you at night or in your thoughts when you're at home, school, or on your job? What important messages has God been giving you? What should you do about them? You should write them down. Document the day and time you had them. Write down the dreams that you've had that God has placed on your mind. Do not neglect them! Cover them in the blood of Jesus that they will come to pass. Ask the Lord for the steps to take with these important messages. Ask the Lord to destroy the terrible ones in Jesus's name! You know what else? Keep dreaming! Keep elaborating on those God-given thoughts. Those dreams will transform into a goal, and that goal into action, and that action into a life you should pursue. So, what are you waiting for? Your destiny awaits you! And it starts with that precious seed—a dream.

Meditate

"Finally, brethren, whatsoever things are true, whatsoever things are honest, whatsoever things are just, whatsoever things are pure, whatsoever things are lovely, whatsoever things are of good report; if there be any virtue, and if there be any praise, think on these things."

Philippians 4:8

"The eyes of your understanding being enlightened; that ye may know what is the hope of his calling, and what the riches of the glory of his inheritance in the saints,"

Ephesians 1:18

"Now unto him that is able to do exceeding abundantly above all that we ask or think, according to the power that worketh in us,"

Ephesians 3:20

Prayer

Dear Father,
Cleanse my mind from any imagination that is not pleasing to you. Please fill my mind with thoughts that come directly from you. Give me dreams each night, Lord. Help me to remember the dreams that I have. Speak to me with dreams and visions that are divine. Use my dreams to reveal to me what I should be doing and what I should stay away from. Give me the grace to recognize your messages. Cover my dreams, thoughts and visions in the blood of Jesus. Thank You. In Jesus's mighty name, amen.

_____

_____

_____

_____

_____

_____

_____

_____

_____

_____

_____

_____

_____

_____

_____

_____

_____

_____

_____

_____

_____

_____

_____

_____

_____

_____

_____

_____

_____

_____

_____

_____

_____

_____

_____

_____

_____

_____

_____

_____

_____

_____

_____

_____

_____

_____

_____

_____

_____

_____

_____

_____

_____

_____

_____

_____

_____

_____

_____

_____

_____

_____

_____

_____

_____

_____

_____

_____

_____

_____

_____

_____

_____

_____

_____

_____

_____

_____

_____

_____

_____

_____

_____

_____

_____

_____

_____

_____

_____

_____

_____

_____

_____

_____

_____

_____

_____

Prayer for a Purpose

"Thou art worthy, O Lord, to receive glory and honour and power: for thou hast created all things, and for thy pleasure they are and were created." Revelation 4:11

Today's Scripture Reading:
Romans 8:28-31; Jeremiah 29:11-13 and Psalms 139

Jesus created us to feel needed and wanted. He made us to have the desire to feel useful. He gave every single one of us needs and talents for His work and glory.

We all have been created by God, for God, and for HIS PURPOSE. Often, when we pursue paths that are not our own, we are left empty. If we are created for God and for His purpose, that means He has a specific plan for our lives, and only He knows the blueprint. We need to ask Him about the specifics of His plans for our lives. Why should we spend the rest of our lives pursuing something the Lord did not call us to do, only to end up unsuccessful and unhappy? Or worse, missing out on our holy destiny? There might be things that your parents, friends and relatives are talking you into doing.

Perhaps they are encouraging you to become a doctor, lawyer, nurse, singer, actor, and so on. Now, I'm not saying these are bad professions, but they may not be what the Lord is calling you to do. He may be calling you to be a painter, to paint the visions of heaven that He may reveal to you. Or, perhaps, He's calling you to be a songwriter to write songs that would alleviate the pain of others. Or He may be calling you to be a doctor to heal His people. The point here is: what is the Lord telling YOU to do?

God's calling may not be what your earthly father is telling you to do or what your friends are suggesting that you do, or even what your professor thinks you should do. But what is the Lord specifically telling you? Although the Lord may use these people to give ideas or guide you, make sure always to seek and ask God if that is the right path first.

In some instances, when you deviate from the Lord, He will allow your life to be frustrated until you are back on His plan. This is like Jonah, who got swallowed by the big fish because he refused to go to Nineveh and complete the Lord's will of preaching to the people (Jonah 1:17; 3:3). In other instances, or after repeated events of trying to get you to stay on the right road, the Lord will let you do what you want apart from His will, inevitably leading to straying away from Him. This often leads to problems in your life. Sadly, this is the fate of many. Due to this sad reality, many are called, but few are chosen (Matthew 22:14). This is the reason why it is important to know the calling the Lord has for your life and to follow the necessary instructions from the Lord to keep on the right track and fulfill your God-given purpose. Rest assured that if the Lord has called you, trust and believe in Him that you will be successful. He will provide the necessary resources, people, and anointing to see you through the end. "He who started a good work in you is faithful to see you through the end" (Philippians 1:6). He is the author and finisher of your faith (Hebrews 12:2).

What is the Lord telling you to do? This could be through a dream, prophecy, or His speaking directly to you. The Lord talks to us in different ways, and due to our own personal relationship with Him, we recognize and understand Him. Talk to the Lord so that He can tell you and confirm it. And pursue that destiny in Jesus's Name! Write down what the Lord has called you to do. Write down your purpose!

Meditate

"For in him we live, and move, and have our being; as certain also of your own poets have said, For we are also his offspring."

Acts 17:28

"Moreover whom he did predestinate, them he also called: and whom he called, them he also justified: and whom he justified, them he also glorified."

Romans 8:30

"For by him were all things created, that are in heaven, and that are in earth, visible and invisible, whether they be thrones, or dominions, or principalities, or powers: all things were created by him, and for him: And he is before all things, and by him all things consist."

Colossians 1:16

Prayer

Dear Heavenly Father,
Thank you for creating me for your own purpose and glory. Reveal to me, Lord, my destiny and the holy plan that you have for my life. Cause me to walk in the steps you have anointed and ordained for my life. Thank you for revealing my purpose. Please protect my destiny in the blood of Jesus Christ. In Jesus's mighty name. Amen.

_____

_____

_____

_____

_____

_____

_____

_____

_____

_____

_____

_____

_____

_____

_____

_____

_____

_____

_____

_____

_____

_____

_____

_____

_____

_____

_____

_____

_____

_____

_____

_____

_____

_____

_____

_____

_____

_____

_____

_____

The Most Important Guest

"But as many as received Him, to them He gave the right to become children of God, even to those who believe in His name." John 1:12

Today's Scripture Reading:
John 1:6-18; Matthew 11:28-30

I have a friend who, whenever there is a group outing, I must tell him, "You're invited." I would say, "Hey, we're all going to so and so's house for this and that." Afterward, he would always ask, "Am I invited?" It was a little annoying. I would always wonder why he would ask that every single time if we were all together. I found out he does this because one day, he went with a friend to an event. And because his name wasn't on the list, they wouldn't let him in with his friend. So, since then, it scared him. That is, he is not going to go anywhere he is not personally invited.

It then came to me that this is just how the Lord is. Jesus is such a gentleman that He is never going to just intrude into your business. He will not always invite himself into your life to tell you who not to marry, what new job to take, the career path to pursue, the state to move to, etc. Everyone has free will, and He is not going to force you to do anything. Consequently, He will not infiltrate your life unless YOU give Him that invitation to do so. He will not come into your house and start cleaning and arranging furniture unless you ask Him to. Although He loves you and wants the best for you in everything, the best choice for your life is subject to your free will, which we all have.

How will anyone know to attend your special moments in life if they are not invited? That should be the same understanding with our Father Jesus. He cares so much about you that He wants to know the special details of your plans. He wants to know what you want to wear that day, what you are planning on eating. He will even give you His opinion if you ask Him.

You must invite the Lord by reverencing Him. Ask Him to come into your heart daily to cleanse your soul, mind and spirit. Ask the Lord with an earnest heart to be a part of everything you do. Once you invite Him, your heart must be open toward His plans for you. Reverencing Him also means opening your wounds to Him, your hurt, fears, doubts, and struggles. Further, be open to His changes; let Him lead you. He is the best guide you'll ever have, and He will be with you every step of the way (Proverbs 3:6). He is not a friend that is going to lie to you. He will tell you the truth because He is The Truth, and there is no lie found in Him (John 14:6). What better person to have by your side than the Lord Jesus? He is your light (Psalm 119:105)! With everyone who is with you, they may fail you in some way or another. They may let you down simply because they are human. However, the Father will never fail you.

As much as you want the Lord to be invited into your life, He wants you to be a part of His life, too (Philippians 1:7), the good and the ugly. It is His desire for you to partake in His great banquet (Luke 14:15). How do you do this? By accepting Jesus Christ as your personal Lord and Savior. Being baptized with the Holy Spirit, indulging yourself in the Word of God, praying, worshiping the Lord, attending a Bible-based church that teaches the true Word of Christ. The Lord is your biggest supporter, but you must draw closer to Him so that he can draw closer to you (James 4:8).

Who is on your guest list? Who are the people you know in your heart are going to be right there with you during your greatest achievements? I hope with all those people that you do not forget THE MOST important guest of them all: your Father Jesus.

What are the ways that you can invite Christ into your life? What areas are you inviting Christ to come into your life? What testimonies have you had since then? Write them down to remember His goodness in your life.

Meditate

"Since you have accepted Christ Jesus as Lord, live in union with him. Keep your roots deep in him, build your lives on him, and become stronger in your faith, as you were taught. And be filled with thanksgiving."

Colossians 2:6-7

"It is through faith that all of you are God's children in union with Christ Jesus. You were baptized into union with Christ, and now you are clothed, so to speak, with the life of Christ himself."

Galatians 3:26-27

"Whosoever shall confess that Jesus is the Son of God, God dwelleth in him, and he in God."

1 John 4:15

Prayer

Dear Jesus,
Thank You for always wanting to be a part of my life. Please forgive me for keeping You out of my life. Father, I invite You into my heart and I invite you to be a part of all my achievements and in all that I do. Come into my heart and heal me of my wounds, fears, and struggles. I invite you to change my heart and my life. Father, I accept You as my personal Lord and Savior. In Jesus's mighty name, amen.

_____

_____

_____

_____

_____

_____

_____

_____

_____

_____

_____

_____

_____

_____

_____

_____

_____

_____

_____

Obedience is Better...

"Behold, I stand at the door, and knock: if any man hear my voice, and open the door, I will come in to him, and will sup with him, and he with me." Revelation 3:20

Today's Scripture Reading:
Deuteronomy 28

As human beings, our fleshly nature always feels the need to be independent. We want to be our own boss, doing everything in our own time and at our own will. This is not a terrible mindset to have if God blesses you with your own business; however, this is a detrimental mindset to have, considering your Father Jesus in heaven. Like a parent, an older sibling, caregiver or supervisor, you want the best for those you are leading or taking care of. Those under you are learning from you because they do not know everything, so they must be taught. When they go the wrong way or do the wrong thing, you guide them correctly.

What if they weren't listening to you? You would be very disappointed because you understand why they shouldn't be doing certain activities that may bring negative consequences as a leader or mentor. This is the same way our Father feels toward us. He is the shepherd of our lives, and what a great shepherd we do have! A shepherd that wants the best for us (Jeremiah 29:11). He knows the beginning and end of our lives. He knows the future (Hebrews 12:2)! He knows what will happen if we choose that particular job or attend that particular school. He knows that if you accept that promotion, the type of stress that would come along with it, and He actually has a better one in store for you if you would just yield, be patient, and obey Him.

Obeying the Lord is so difficult for us because we want to do what seems right to us (Proverbs 14:12). However, this is not always the best for our lives. Disobeying the Lord is the same as rebellion and participating in witchcraft (1 Samuel 15:23). When an individual does not obey God, that person makes themselves a god, serving themselves and their desires. That person will then become an idol, and the Lord cannot work with that. The Lord Jesus cannot work with idolatry, and with that, there is no room for the Holy Spirit to penetrate their heart and speak concerning the best plans He has for their life for His glory. As we disobey the Lord, we push the Holy Spirit away from us because disobedience is sin. The Holy Spirit and sin just don't mix. When you sin, there is a hedge broken for the enemy to enter your life and do what he has to do with you since disobedience is an attribute of his. Yielding to Satan is the same as giving him permission to do his will in your life.

During their exodus period out of Egypt, the Israelites served as an example of disobedience to the Lord. In their case, what would have taken 40 days to get to the promised land took forty years since they did not yield to the Lord! Another example of delay due to disobedience is when the Israelites lost their land under siege to a foreign nation after years of God's patience and chances. The Lord had so much in store for them, including sustaining their nation, if they would have just obeyed. On numerous occasions, the Lord commanded and warned them to obey His commandments; however, they never listened, and the negative outcome concerning their lives was fulfilled. It was not worth it for them to lose their blessings just to appease their sinful lusts.

If you cannot obey the Lord in the little things, will you obey Him concerning more jeopardizing situations? You must get into the habit of obeying the Lord now so that you may hear Him clearly considering important decisions in your life. Remember, the Holy Spirit intervenes for you and tells you vital information because He cares for you. Alternately, if you do not listen to Him, you may fall prey to a problem that could have been avoided. I have made so many bad decisions, such as joining myself in programs and groups that the Lord told me not to. As a result, things turned out badly for me. Thank God for His grace and mercy that He was still able to turn those bad decisions around and make them work for my good. Nevertheless, OBEDIENCE IS BETTER THAN SACRIFICE (1 Samuel 15:22).

You do not want to make unwise decisions. For example, you do not want to decide to marry the wrong person and start seeing red flags later. The Holy Spirit saw it, and He tried to warn you. He tugged at your heart many times, but you didn't listen. Now you are dealing with a divorce. Now you are stuck with the pieces of a broken heart. That was almost my story. Perhaps it was a town He told you not to move to. He warned you, but you didn't listen, and now your house is undergoing foreclosure for a myriad of reasons. Or, maybe He told you not to take that business deal with that company. You signed anyway, and you found out that the company was financially faulty and is now laying off many of its workers, including you.

Disobeying the Lord has detrimental consequences,

including a delay to your destiny. The Lord will still sustain you with His grace, but that entire ordeal and starting over could have been avoided because He told you. The Lord is such a gentleman that he would not advise you over and over but allow you to do what you will. But my love, when you make that decision, you will wish you never did.

One day when I was in church, the Lord told me to fast out of the blue. I said, "Lord, I can't fast because I drank orange juice." He still assured me to take a fast. So, I obeyed, though I questioned it; I still obeyed. I did not eat that entire day. Even as I cooked for my client at work, I didn't taste the food. On my way home, I thought about breaking my fast at midnight. When I was just a block away from my home, a GMC Sierra traveling around 40 miles per hour hit my car! Later, after X-rays, I found out my spine was displaced, leaving me to complete five months of treatment. The collision left the entire front of my car smashed. Imagine if I did not obey the voice of the Lord and went with what I thought was right? This accident could have been much worse. Maybe I could have lost my life. Praises to the Lord because He caused me to listen and He protected me! The Lord says when you hear His voice, harden not your heart toward Him (Hebrews 3:15). Unless you learn to listen to Him, you may never know what the Lord is warning you about and how it could protect your life by making the right decision.

What is the Lord telling you to do concerning your destiny or your present situation? Jot it down. How will you make the necessary steps to obey Him? My love, the consequences are not worth disobeying the Lord. Ask the Lord for His strength and the grace to yield to His voice and do what is right concerning Him.

Meditate

"Jesus answered and said unto him, If a man love me, he will keep my words: and my Father will love him, and we will come unto him, and make our abode with him."

John 14:23

"And it shall come to pass, if thou shalt hearken diligently unto the voice of the Lord thy God, to observe and to do all his commandments which I command thee this day, that the Lord thy God will set thee on high above all nations of the earth:"

Deuteronomy 28:1

"This book of the law shall not depart out of thy mouth; but thou shalt meditate therein day and night, that thou mayest observe to do according to all that is written therein: for then thou shalt make thy way prosperous, and then thou shalt have good success."

Joshua 1:8

Prayer

Dear Father,
I love You dearly, and I don't want to disappoint You. I want Your best for my life. Open my heart to hearing Your voice. Father, give me Your grace and strength to yield and obey You. Lord, let me recognize Your voice. In Jesus's name, amen.

_____

_____

_____

_____

_____

_____

_____

_____

_____

_____

_____

_____

_____

_____

_____

_____

_____

_____

_____

_____

_____

_____

_____

_____

_____

_____

_____

_____

_____

_____

_____

_____

_____

_____

_____

_____

_____

_____

_____

_____

_____

_____

_____

_____

_____

_____

_____

_____

_____

_____

_____

_____

_____

_____

_____

_____

_____

_____

_____

Covenant-Keeping God

"The Lord is not slack concerning his promise, as some men count slackness; but is longsuffering to usward, not willing that any should perish, but that all should come to repentance." 2 Peter 3:9

Today's Scripture Reading:
Psalm 105:8-11

When I was young, my dad always used to promise that we were going to the Mall of America. Repeatedly, he would tell me that, and each time I would jump up and down with excitement at the announcement. "Daddy is taking me to the mall today! Daddy said, 'We are going to the mall!'" However, each time he said that we would never go. He would say, "Later," or "Tomorrow." And with each time, I would become more and more disappointed. I accepted the fact that we would never go to the mall, and we never did. From that time on, I never took anything he said to heart. I would just brush it off to save myself from further disappointment and heartbreak.

This was not the first time he disappointed me, and it was not the last.

My father is not the only person who has disappointed me; many others have done the same. This might be the case for you where others have made promises they could not keep. If you're like me, the most heartbreaking was your father's broken promises. You might even feel that way toward your Heavenly Father. He has promised you something, but you have been waiting, or you feel that it's passed you by. You've been continuously praying, yet you see no results. Maybe you've been in the same situation for years now and nothing seems to be changing. Your faith is shaking, and you're on the verge of doing something you're not supposed to, to alleviate the pain, to get you out of that struggle. You feel that the Lord has forgotten you. He has forgotten the vow that was made between the two of you.

The Lord is not slack concerning his promises, as some people are. Sweetheart, He did not forget, and He has not forgotten about you. He is still watching over you and working on your behalf. Just because you can't see it does not mean He is not moving for you. He has angels working on your behalf and completing all that needs to be done. The supernatural time that God operates on is different from our physical time (2 Peter 3:8). What has been completed in the spiritual is still being manifested in the physical. My love, what the Lord has started in you, He is faithful to complete within you (Philippians 1:6).

God knows you. He knows your heart's desires. Who you were going to be was not hidden from Him when He created you (Psalm 139:15). He is always with you wherever you go (Psalm 139:8). He knows how many hairs you have on your head (Luke 12:7). So, why wouldn't He know or forget the promises made concerning your life? He sees your heartbreak. He knows the nights when you cry, and He has kept every tear in a bottle (Psalm 56:8). That's how much He cares for you.

Darling, you serve a God who loves you and makes covenants with His people. Because of His Word and how powerful His promises are, nothing can break them. That is why the Lord loves making vows with His people because it serves as a protection contract, and Satan cannot penetrate that particular area of your life. It must come to pass! Satan might try to fight against you in that aspect of your life to shake your faith, but don't give in! Once that covenant is made, it cannot be broken. The Lord made a covenant with my mother that all her children would be well taken care of. And it has come to pass, as the Lord is always fighting on my behalf and that of my siblings. My brother did not lose his life while serving in the Marines; neither did he lose his life to cancer, although the enemy fought for his life on several occasions. After many events of my sister almost losing her life in the streets, it never happened. Against all odds of fighting four years of depression, the Lord still saw me through graduating university. I praise the Lord for that covenant of protection He made with my mother concerning our lives.

From the Scripture reading, we can see just a few of the promises that the Lord kept with His children. For instance, He promised the children of Israel the land of Canaan, and despite their rebellion against God, they inhabited the land. God promised that He would build a house for David. He also promised that David's son, Solomon, would build the house of the Lord, and it came to pass. He promised Abraham's wife, Sarah, a son in her old age. As He promised, she conceived and gave birth to Isaac. He promised the coming of the Messiah, Immanuel, His own self in the flesh. Even though Satan made many attempts to stop Him from coming and staying on this earth to die for our sins, that covenant was still fulfilled. He promised not to flood the earth again with water, and the rainbow is a symbol of that covenant that He made with the world. These are just a few promises that have manifested. This tells us that the covenants and promises made for our lives would manifest this same way!

If men who are wicked can give good gifts to their children, what more about our Father God, who is Holy (Matthew 7:11)? He is able and willing to go above and beyond more than you can ever imagine. Trust the Lord.

If God is able to make a covenant with you and follow through, make sure you honor whatever vow that you make with the Lord. He counts it just as sacred as you do concerning His promises. Do not allow the enemy an open door into your life by even thinking about breaking a vow made between you and your Father. Deliberately breaking your vow is a sin (Ecclesiastes 5:4-6).

What covenant has the Lord made with you? What promises has He made for you and your generations? What would you like to see done in your life from the Father? Journal them here as a testimony when it manifests! Believe in Him; He will always follow through if it is His will for your life.

Meditate

"My covenant I will not violate, Nor will I alter the utterance of My lips."

Psalm 89:34

"He hath given meat unto them that fear him: he will ever be mindful of his covenant."

Psalm 111:5

"And he said, Lord God of Israel, there is no God like thee, in heaven above, or on earth beneath, who keepest covenant and mercy with thy servants that walk before thee with all their heart:"

1 Kings 8:23

"For the mountains may be removed and the hills may shake, But My lovingkindness will not be removed from you, And My covenant of peace will not be shaken, Says the LORD who has compassion on you."

Isaiah 54:10

Prayer

Dear Lord,

Thank You for the covenants and promises that You have made over my life and destiny. You are faithful and just in all that You do. You are faithful concerning covenants. Thank You for fulfilling all the promises that You have over my life, and help me to walk in Your just paths. Lord, I ask that You make a covering for me today. Make a covenant with me concerning my life today. Thank You for Your overpowering mercy and grace. I plead the blood of Jesus over my destiny. In Jesus's mighty name, amen.

_____

_____

_____

_____

_____

_____

_____

_____

_____

_____

_____

_____

_____

_____

_____

_____

_____

_____

Lose Some to Win More

"He that findeth his life shall lose it: and he that loseth his life for my sake shall find it." Matthew 10:39

Today's Scripture Reading:
Matthew 19:16-22; Isaiah 58:1-9a.

Anything that you want in this life will require giving up something meaningful to you. The exchange usually is not easy. This just means that there is a breakthrough to a new level in your life. But how important is it to you? What are you willing to give up, and why?

Take, for example, the scripture reading. The rich man wanted to follow Jesus, but he easily got depressed, thinking about giving up his riches. How badly did he want to follow the Lord? Was he ready to give it all up? He wasn't ready. Think of all that He could've obtained by walking with the Lord, all the anointing and power that He could've been blessed with. His riches in heaven were going to be more than the ones that he had stored here on earth that would fade and deteriorate (Matthew 6:19-20). Where your treasures are, that's where your heart is also (Matthew 6:21). His treasures weren't in heaven, so his heart wasn't there either. They were here on earth because he couldn't seem to let go of his temporary items for something much more valuable, such as Christ. All else he would've been granted. We are all like this rich man, fighting to let go of what is not profitable to receive something much greater. That is the hard exchange we have to make, but nobody can do it FOR you; it is a task that you have to complete yourself, from your heart.

Sacrificing your time and energy up to the Lord is an important and highly effective way not only to get closer to the Lord but also to break those tough chains that just don't want to be broken. I fasted many times during my younger years. But one of the times I fasted that really broke chains was when I was in my first relationship. It was my fourth year of college when I started dating a man that unknowingly was much older than I was. He treated me badly. The relationship tore me down physically, psychologically, emotionally and even spiritually. However, thanks to God, the situation built me instead of breaking me. No matter what he did to me, or how much he embarrassed me in front of the community, family and friends, I was still in love with him and wanted to stay. I was in a toxic soul tie that needed to be broken, but it was too strong. Prayer alone couldn't break it (Mark 9:29)!

Everything around me was going down, so I decided to go before the Lord with a fast. I did a three-day fast with NO FOOD, and just one 16.5 ounce bottle of water every 24 hours. Just one! I indulged in the Word of God, praying constantly. I also had to attend classes and study because it was finals week and I had to work as well. It was tough! But the Lord gave me HIS STRENGTH, and the soul tie was broken! The spiritual attacks subsided, and things around me were lighting up again. The Lord had set me free, and "Who the Son sets free is free indeed (John 8:36)!" I desperately wanted that change.

I needed it because I knew that if I didn't do something fast, the enemy would break me down and try to destroy me and my destiny with those situations. I had to sacrifice food, energy, social time, and sleep to get what my soul yearned for—Freedom and Redemption. Isaiah 58:6 says, "Is not this the fast that I have chosen? To loose the bands of wickedness, to undo the heavy burdens, and to let the oppressed go free, and that ye break every yoke?"

The purpose of a fast is to break bands, chains, boulders, and anything that keeps your spirit, goals, your relationship with God, etc. captive. Don't overlook fasting! Don't think that it is old school—the Lord never changes; His words never fade away (Matthew 24:35). It is vital in fighting against the toughest battles in your life. Fasting and honoring the Lord with sacred time works and has the results to prove it. Fasting for even an hour unto the Lord, He honors that.

In order to receive all the blessings that the Lord wants to give you, you're going to have to let go of that job, that relationship, that particular plan. Fast before Him, so God can give you what was originally promised for you, and much more.

What you're so afraid of giving up is nothing compared to what the Lord has in store for you. For the Lord to get to you to give you what you need, you have to remove that block. What has been on your heart to let go of? What things in your life are hindering you from reaching your full potential through him? Jot them down. Let them go today. Take time before the Lord with prayer and fasting if you feel they are too tough to break. Let those burdens go.

Meditate

"Is not this the fast that I have chosen? To loose the bands of wickedness, to undo the heavy burdens, and to let the oppressed go free, and that ye break every yoke?"

Isaiah 58:6

"Then said Jesus unto his disciples, If any man will come after me, let him deny himself, and take up his cross, and follow me."

Matthew 16:24

"Lay not up for yourselves treasures upon earth, where moth and rust doth corrupt, and where thieves break through and steal: But lay up for yourselves treasures in heaven, where neither moth nor rust doth corrupt, and where thieves do not break through nor steal: For where your treasure is, there will your heart be also."

Matthew 6:19-21

Prayer

Dear Father,

Thank You for all that You have done in my life. Father, I ask that You remove anything that is a hindrance in my life. Please give me your grace and strength to release anything that is holding me back from Your blessing. Release me from anyone or anything that is causing a separation between You and me. Lord, let me give You my burdens and the things in my life that do not please You so that You can exchange it for better. Teach me to fast and give me the strength to fast in honor to You, Lord. Thank You in advance. In Jesus's mighty name. Amen.

_____

_____

_____

_____

_____

_____

_____

_____

_____

_____

_____

_____

_____

_____

_____

_____

_____

_____

_____

Manifest Wisdom

"The fear of the Lord is the beginning of wisdom: and the knowledge of the holy is understanding." Proverbs 9:10

Scripture Reading:
Proverbs 8; 2 Chronicles 1:7-17

One of the components that God used to build this very foundation of the earth was His infinite wisdom (Proverbs 8:23)! The Lord used His wisdom to sustain life.

The enemy is also wise; that is the reason why it is important to tap into the Lord's Godly wisdom to be able to fight and defeat the enemy and his relentless attacks. How we do this is by spending time with the Lord daily, reading His word, listening to the Holy Spirit, asking him to be our guide in everything we do and with every inquiry that we have. Lean not on thy own understanding (Proverbs 3:5b). The Lord instructs us to be as wise as a serpent and as cool as a dove (Matthew 10:16b).

One way the Lord speaks to me and allows me to obtain knowledge is by having me research, through searching the scriptures of His Word, reading other books, or researching via the internet. The Lord wants us to be intelligent, to love wisdom and call her our family (Proverbs 7:4). These days, many people want riches. They want to get rich quick, but that doesn't always hold. However, wisdom is a foundation that is there to build, sustain and grow. You can pass it on to others, teach, and whatever you learn will stick with you for a lifetime.

King Solomon knew that one of the keys to being a great leader was wisdom. For this reason, when the Father asked him what he would like, he told the Lord he wanted wisdom and knowledge. Since he did not ask for money but wisdom, which pleased the Lord, God gave him wisdom, knowledge, wealth and riches beyond anyone! Beyond what any king would ever receive! God was so pleased with what Solomon asked for because the Lord honors wisdom! Proverbs 8:35 says, "For whoso findeth me (wisdom) findeth life, and shall obtain favour of the Lord." Since Solomon searched and asked for wisdom, the Lord favored him and gave him more blessings unexpectedly.

Wisdom will keep you going in the right direction, aid you with creativity, and aid you in choosing the right people to have around you, the right advice to give, and the people and activities to stay away from. Wisdom keeps you out of trouble and moving along the path that is best for your life. According to Proverbs 8:1-5, wisdom is crying out for people to seek and find her. This is because, through sound wisdom, life is found. The Word of God states, "My people are destroyed for lack of knowledge (Hosea 4:6a)." Think of how many people are getting into things and signing up for things they know nothing about! Many of the skills you have can be enhanced by studying and seeking knowledge. In the end, many people end up losing what they could have gained because they didn't take the time to research and obtain wisdom from the Father.

You cannot serve God properly without wisdom (Hosea 4:6). My love, you can't walk in your destiny without wisdom. Wisdom is an attribute of God and fearing and reverencing the Lord is how you obtain that wisdom and more of it. It is a science! A holy pathway. After all, it is the Lord who brings revelation to you. So, if you are not reverencing Him and spending time with Him, how will you retrieve those messages? It amazes me that people can distinguish between their favorite musicians' voices when they come on the radio but not the Lord's voice. That is because you spend time with them by meditating on their music. It is important to stick to the Lord. Hear what He has to say concerning your life and collect all the wisdom you can from Him. "For the LORD giveth wisdom: out of his mouth cometh knowledge and understanding" (Proverbs 2:6).

Where is it that you want the Lord to give you wisdom? Jot it down. Remember, all that we learn here is just earthy wisdom. What about Godly, holy wisdom? Don't forget to think of ways that you would like to learn more about the Lord and His word and what He can reveal to you. Let wisdom manifest in your life.

Meditate

"For wisdom is better than rubies; and all things that may be desired are not to be compared to it."

Proverbs 8:11

"For whoso findeth me findeth life, and shall obtain favour of the Lord. But he that sinneth against me wrongeth his own soul: all they that hate me love death."

Proverbs 8:35,36

"The fear of the Lord is the beginning of wisdom: a good understanding have all they that do his commandments: his praise endureth for ever."

Psalm 111:10

"For by me thy days shall be multiplied, and the years of thy life shall be increased."

Proverbs 9:11

Prayer

Dear Father,

I come to You to ask You for Your abundant wisdom. I ask You for Your knowledge and Your understanding. Lord, let me receive knowledge in Your Word, wisdom in being a leader, wisdom in my everyday life, and everything that is aligned with my destiny. Thank You, Lord, for answering my prayer by faith. In Jesus's mighty name, amen.

Giving to Receive

"He who has a generous eye will be blessed, for he gives his bread to the poor." Proverbs 22:9 NKJV

Today's Scripture Reading:
Matthew 19:16-26; Matthew 25:34-46

The Lord has called us to serve (Matthew 20:26). He has called us to serve Him and to serve one another. In all your endeavors in which you excel, remember to give to those who are less fortunate. The Lord will hold you accountable when you turn a blind eye to those in need (Proverbs 28:27), especially when He has blessed you abundantly to give.

From the time of being a high school student spanning through my college years, life was difficult for my family and me. My father wasn't active in our lives, and my mother had lost her job. This led to our family losing to foreclosure our childhood home, which we lived in for 18 years! My mother and younger brother were then homeless and lacked financially.

Even growing up, my family and I were very humble, poor.

My mother was single, trying to make ends meet with four kids. Even with that, my mother always gave to those in need, even though we were in need ourselves. As much as my mother gave, God sent others to give to us also. Where would we have been if we didn't have those people that God sent to us to bless us financially, giving clothes, food, and other care items when we had nothing? It is important to think that way and be that same light for others.

As you go and become successful, and the Lord blesses you financially, don't turn your face from those in need (Proverbs 22:9). Help out in any way the Lord places on your heart. Food pantries, donating to those in need, scholarships, sponsor a child! Let God use us to raise up another generation of giving hands.

If giving is your area of struggle, talk to the Lord to help you and give you that heart of giving. He loves a cheerful giver; let it come from the heart (2 Corinthians 9:7). One reason it is hard for a rich man or woman to enter the Kingdom of God is because of his heart for not giving. The heart of holding all your possessions to yourself will cause you to lose your blessings and the Kingdom of God. However, with all this, it is possible with God. He will help you (Matthew 19:21-26).

The Lord gave His life to us freely. So then, what is so difficult about giving up material gains such as cars, clothes, money, or even something as simple as food? The devil may lie to you and say, "If you give, what will you have for yourself? How will you take care of your family?" But my love, that is a LIE. There have been many times in my life where I didn't have enough, and the Lord urged me to give what little that I had, and I got blessed the most! I never ran out of food; I was well kept, and the Lord always blessed me with what I needed! Even with little, it was honestly a miracle. You need to trust Him and allow the Lord to work in your life so you can have a testimony!

When you give a hand to those who are less fortunate—clothe, feed, visit those who are brokenhearted, offer love with your actions—you have done it unto the Lord Jesus (Matthew 25:40). The Lord demonstrated with His life that he came for the poor. His heart is always toward those in poverty, the brokenhearted and the oppressed. And He is always fighting their battles (Proverbs 22:22-23). Giving isn't always monetary. You can give your TIME to those in need as well. Make a meal for someone who you know may have no food. Bless them with prayer, a shoulder to cry on, a hand to hold. Just being with someone and offering emotional support may change their feeling of hopelessness (Proverbs 27:9). Sometimes, someone may just need a soul to be with them.

If you see someone in need of emotional support or in need generally, don't just turn your face and think, "Someone will help them later; I don't have time right now." If you have the time to give or the resources, give what is needed (Proverbs 3:28; James 2:15,16). Also, when you do these things for others, don't do it for recognition or what you can receive back from them, but do it out of purity and because it is the will and commandment of God. Know that your reward will be greater in heaven and the Lord will bless you accordingly. You will receive your reward from the Father (Matthew 6:4).

The Lord will reveal to you many unique ways that you can help others, designed specifically for you to do! Assigned directly for you! Jot down ways the Lord is calling you to contribute your gifts. What is He directing you to do to be of service to others? Write it down. It's time to start building up the kingdom of heaven. We all want the Lord to say, "Well done thy good and faithful servant." Don't let all the gifts the Lord has given you go in vain!

Meditate

"Every man according as he purposeth in his heart, so let him give; not grudgingly, or of necessity: for God loveth a cheerful giver."

2 Corinthians 9:7

"Whoso stoppeth his ears at the cry of the poor, he shall cry himself, but shall not be heard."

Proverbs 21:13

"But when thou doest alms, let not thy left hand know what thy right hand doeth: That thine alms may be in secret: and thy Father which seeth in secret himself shall reward thee openly."

Matthew 6:3,4

Prayer

Dear Lord, thank You for revealing Your heart to me. Thank You for all the times that You have provided for me and taken care of me. Lord, give me a heart of giving. Lord, convict my heart with the Holy Spirit to help anyone who may be in lack. Give me Your eyes so that I may see your people the way You see them. Give me Your heart that I may love your people the way You love them. Give me a heart for the poor and oppressed. I want to be a cheerful giver. Let me give all alms in purity. Thank You, Lord. In Jesus's name, amen.

_____

_____

_____

_____

_____

_____

_____

_____

_____

_____

_____

_____

_____

_____

_____

_____

_____

_____

Live without Fear

"For I the LORD thy God will hold thy right hand, saying unto thee, Fear not; I will help thee." Isaiah 41:13

Today's Scripture Reading:
Joshua chapter 1, Isaiah 41: 8-17

The biggest enemy to you and your progression in life is fear. Fear will cause you not to move where God has called you to be. Fear will have you not stand up amongst others because of how others might view you. I was afraid to write this book because I thought, "God, I'm not perfect; I am not worthy. There are so many things I've done that I am not proud of; what if people judge me?" However, God commanded me to write this book because of the lives He is sending this book to minister to. Fear will have you disobey God by plaguing you with your insecurities. However, it is not just about YOU, but what GOD WANTS you to do. This is about how God is going to use your story, your life, to bless others and build His kingdom. The kingdom of God is dependent on our prosperity in life. Disobedience through the medium of fear will cause us not to walk in the prosperous life we were meant to receive.

Satan uses fear to cripple us and, in turn, reject the plan that God has for us. Satan uses fear to speak to our minds to tell us we are not worthy enough. Fear will tell us that we don't have the skills, money, experience, or dedication to complete that which we need to do. If we are not careful, fear can become an idol in our lives. Listening to fear and not listening to God can cause us to be rebellious against God, hurting not only our destiny but our Father as well.

How do we defeat fear so that we walk in the will of the Father? We do this by communing with the Lord, spending time with Him in His word and prayer. Reading the Word of God, you will be able to see how those before us overcame their fear through the power of God. Spending time in prayer will enable us to bring to God what worries us. Through prayer, He will then replace that fear with courage and give us the strength we need to accomplish His will. Spending time with the Lord will provide you with the inner confidence you need to shine and succeed. When the spirit of fear is coming over me, I actually speak out of my mouth and say, "Spirit of fear, I cast you out in the name of Jesus! You have no power over me!" With the authority that your Father Jesus gave you, you have the authority to cast out these spirits (Luke 10:19).

God has not given you the spirit of fear, but He has given you that of a sound mind and love (2 Timothy 1:7). FEAR is not from God but from the devil whose constant goal is to cripple God by crippling his loved creation—His people.

Imagine if Jesus listened to the spirit of fear when it was time for Him to die on the cross, we wouldn't have the gift of salvation! If He had let fear enter in, He would not have completed the will of God. In our scripture reading, Joshua was the new leader of Israel after the death of Moses. God told Him that He should not be afraid (Joshua 1:9), but he should be of good courage and strong, and he and the people should obey the commandments of the Lord (Joshua 1:18). Joshua could not let fear overtake him or be fearful because that would have hindered him in the task of bringing Gods' people into the promised land. With such a task, he needed God's guidance and strength to complete it, and fear would've dismantled the plan that God had.

You cannot serve God and fear at the same time. There is nothing to fear when the battle is God's (2 Chronicles 20:15). The Lord is always with you, holding your hand to get you through (Isaiah 41:13). The creator of the universe, the Lord of Hosts (armies), is your guide, your Father. You are victorious; you already have the victory. You have no reason to fear!

We are called to do the will of God, but we cannot serve God in the way He needs with fear holding us back. We need to let go of those fears and give them to God so He can give us the strength and confidence we need to serve Him and live life in the prosperity He has called us to live in. What fears do you have regarding what God has called you to do? Write down all your fears, doubts, anxieties and worries on a separate piece of paper. Lay your hands over the paper and pray over it with the prayer on the next page. When you're done praying, rip up that sheet into pieces. You are no longer bound to those fears! Walk confidently in the Lord in all your endeavors!

Meditate

"I sought the LORD, and he heard me, and delivered me from all my fears."

Psalm 34:4

"Then shalt thou prosper, if thou takest heed to fulfil the statutes and judgments which the LORD charged Moses with concerning Israel: be strong, and of good courage; dread not, nor be dismayed."

1 Chronicles 22:13

"For God hath not given us the spirit of fear; but of power, and of love, and of a sound mind."

2 Timothy 1:7

Prayer

Father, in the name of Jesus, I cast the spirit of fear out of my life! I plead the blood of Jesus over this paper as a weapon to destroy all those fears that would hinder Your plan for my life, Lord. Father, take captive every unfruitful thought and cast it out of my mind and spirit. Lord, eliminate each subject of worry, fear and anxiety written on this paper. Lord Jesus, as I rip up this paper, through Your power, all these distractions will be destroyed in the mighty name of Jesus! Thank You for Your power; thank You for this new journey of life with no fear. Lord, put in me Your courage, strength, confidence, and power. I bless You, Lord. In Jesus's name, amen.

Hand to the Plow

"But Jesus answered them, My Father worketh hitherto, and I work." John 5:17

Today's Scripture Reading:
Matthew 25:14-30; 2 Thessalonians 3:6-10; Ephesians 5:15-17

During parts of my school career, I was really spoiled. God spoiled me with so much favor with my teachers that I reached a point where I started slacking. Sometimes, when I wasn't prepared for an exam, I would pray for an extreme blizzard. It would snow, and school would actually be canceled the day of my exam! I then started abusing God's grace on my life and began to procrastinate and be extremely lazy.

Instead of studying, I would take a nap or hang out and eat with my friends. Brothers and sisters, I was wrong for doing that! I was wrong for abusing the favor and grace of God. The Bible instructs us that we should do all things for the glory of God (1 Corinthians 10:31). I wasn't using the favor He was giving me for His glory, but for mine. I thought that since God always came to my rescue, I could do whatever I wanted, and He would come to my rescue again. Instead of using His grace productively, I was using it for my own benefit. I learned terrible lessons from these experiences countless times because there were times my teachers would give me no mercy, and I would fail that assignment or even the class!

As you read in scripture, the master (God) blessed each person with a certain amount of money (talent), which was supposed to be multiplied. Those who multiplied, God was well pleased with and made rulers over many things. And he who did not multiply, God took the talent from and cast him out. To whom much is given, much is required (Luke 12:48).

God does not give us these gifts just to waste them and be lazy. God is not lazy! He is a God that never sleeps (Psalm 121:3-4)! If God took a nap, do you think any of us would be living? Angels work extra hard to take care of us and the kingdom of darkness also works extra hard to destroy us! The Word of God even admires the ants that are so tiny but work so hard (Proverbs 6:6-8). So why would you sleep on your destiny? Your own laziness can destroy your destiny (Proverbs 22:33-34). You cannot be effective in the place that God is taking you if you are lazy or procrastinate. God cannot use you effectively for His kingdom if you spend all your time on social media or sleeping all day. You have to match vision with action, faith with works (James 2:17). Our Father cannot entrust you with bigger tasks that lead to bigger blessings if you can't even complete the few that He has given you. You must put in work to fulfill your God-given purpose on this earth and to reach heaven. Whatever purpose God has given you, just know that it would involve your hard work and strength. Do not let laziness waste the grace, favor, and gifts that God has given you.

Write down the areas in your life where you are struggling with laziness. In what areas in your life are you struggling because of procrastination? Write it down. After praying, come back and write down the instructions that God gave you to combat these struggles. You can revisit this section and write down more solutions at any time.

Meditate

"And Jesus said unto him, No man, having put his hand to the plough, and looking back, is fit for the kingdom of God."

Luke 9:62

"Whatsoever thy hand findeth to do, do it with thy might; for there is no work, nor device, nor knowledge, nor wisdom, in the grave, whither thou goest."

Ecclesiastes 9:10

"He that is faithful in that which is least is faithful also in much: and he that is unjust in the least is unjust also in much."

Luke 16:10

"He who has a slack hand becomes poor, But the hand of the diligent makes rich."

Proverbs 10:4

Prayer

Dear Father, give me Your strength to overcome my weaknesses. I declare in the name of Jesus; I am no longer lazy! I declare in the name of Jesus; I am no longer a procrastinator! I will fulfill my destiny with the power of Jesus Christ! Father, give me Your strength to work hard to fulfill Your purpose for my life. Reveal to me where I fall short and give me the grace to cancel those attributes in my life. Help me to succeed in You. Please give me unmeasurable favor and grace to succeed that I will not abuse. Thank You, Lord. I seal this prayer in the mighty blood of Jesus. In Jesus's name, amen.

_____

_____

_____

_____

_____

_____

_____

_____

_____

_____

_____

_____

_____

_____

_____

_____

_____

_____

_____

_____

_____

_____

_____

_____

_____

_____

_____

_____

_____

_____

_____

_____

_____

_____

_____

_____

_____

_____

No Ghost but the Holy Ghost

"Do not cast me away from Your presence, And do not take Your Holy Spirit from me." Psalm 51:11

Today's Scripture Reading:
1 Corinthians 2:9-14; 1 Corinthians 12:4-11

Truly, the greatest gift that God has blessed us with was the shedding of His innocent blood on Calvary for our sins—gracing us with salvation. When the Lord ascended into heaven, He left with each of us the Holy Spirit (John 14:16). Do you hear that voice that tells you when you're doing something wrong? Yes, that is the Holy Spirit. The Holy Spirit can keep your physical life out of danger and your spirit man from being spiritually dead. Without the Holy Spirit, you cannot function to the utmost in your Spirit-filled, best life.

Just as we need food to survive, we need the word of God to live. When we don't eat, our bodies become weak, we don't obtain the needed nutrients, and eventually, over long periods of time of not eating, we die. It is the same with spiritual food, which is the word of God. This is why we need the Holy Spirit.

The Holy Spirit interprets the word of God for us and gives us understanding. The Holy Spirit also gives us instructions. We need to eat and digest those instructions and live by them! If we don't have the Lord speaking to us, our lives result in spiritual death.

"But he answered and said, It is written, Man shall not live by bread alone, but by every word that proceedeth out of the mouth of God."-Matthew 4:4

The Holy Spirit is our sustaining life force. Without Him, we cannot stay connected to the Father or have a relationship with Him. The Holy Spirit keeps us on the right path in our life and with God. He leads our direction (Psalm 119:105) to righteousness and our purpose in this life. When He tells us something and we disobey Him, we quench Him. The Holy Spirit is an ignited fire within us (Hebrews 12:29). So, when we disobey Him, we start to quench His flame within us (1 Thessalonians 5:19). When we sin, we grieve the Holy Spirit and that also can quench His flame within us (Ephesians 4:30). Our bodies are the temple of the Holy Spirit (1 Corinthians 6:19-20). He does not live in a church building, but He resides in our living, moving bodies. Our bodies are His home. If we are consumed with sin, He has to leave because light and darkness physically cannot stay together. Those are two different elements (2 Corinthians 6:14). The Holy Spirit is power! The Kingdom of God is made up of the backbone of the Holy Spirit and His power (Romans 14:17). The Holy Spirit is what keeps the Kingdom of God active and functioning. He is the powerhouse.

The Holy Spirit is a teacher (1 John 2:27). He is a giver of various gifts, freely giving to all as He pleases (1 Corinthians 12:7,11). The Holy Spirit comforts you (John 14:26). The Holy Spirit is the living water that quenches our everlasting thirst when we are connected to and planted in the Holy Spirit (John 7:37-39). As living water, He waters us. We do not wither, and everything we do prospers (Psalms 1:3).

The powerful Holy Spirit is a giver of gifts, a consuming fire, a comforter, a friend to us, and so much more. Commune and stay close with Him.

Meditate on all the scriptures listed on this day, including the references in the text. What scriptures stand out to you the most? What is the Holy Spirit speaking and revealing to you about Himself? Write them down. Allow the Holy Spirit to be active in your life.

Meditate

"Blessed *And he humbled thee, and suffered thee to hunger, and fed thee with manna, which thou knewest not, neither did thy fathers know; that he might make thee know that man doth not live by bread only, but by every word that proceedeth out of the mouth of the* LORD *doth man live.*"

Deuteronomy 8:3

"Thy *But the Comforter, which is the Holy Ghost, whom the Father will send in my name, he shall teach you all things, and bring all things to your remembrance, whatsoever I have said unto you.*"

John 14:26

"Do Now *the God of hope fill you with all joy and peace in believing, that ye may abound in hope, through the power of the Holy Ghost.*"

Romans 15:13

Prayer

Dear Lord, I thank You for your Holy Spirit. Fill me with the living water of Your word. Consume anything that is within me that is not of You. Teach me to do God's will and fulfill my purpose. Speak into my life. Lord, turn me into a tree of righteousness that flourishes and prospers. I invite You to be a friend in my life. I ask all these things of You. In Jesus's mighty name, amen.

Resist the Devil

"Submit yourselves therefore to God. Resist the devil, and he will flee from you." James 4:7

Today's Scripture Reading:
Matthew 4:1-11, Ephesians 6:12-18

Do you ever wonder why when you're walking down the right path, doing the right thing, that your old life and old bad habits start tugging at you? They pull and pull at you until you finally give in and find yourself back at phase one. This is the most common tactic that the enemy uses to knock you off your feet. If this doesn't ruin you, then he uses this tactic to slow you down in your progress and spiritual life.

When you're making progress by sticking close to God, submitting to His will and getting your goals accomplished, Satan has a way of coming in and tempting you to destruction. Three months before my first marriage anniversary, the devil had been attacking me spiritually. Every night for two weeks, he showed me dreams, tormenting me with sin that he wanted me to partake, trying to tempt me with sins of my old life, and threatening to take my husband away from me. He even tried to take the life of my husband and me! Since I made a conscious decision to stick with the Lord, the devil was disappointed that he could not get me to sin in my physical life. He then wanted to taint my mind and spirit by defiling my dreams. Each time this would happen, I would wake up and pray out loud! I would cancel the dream, and I would declare out loud that that was not my life anymore. I spoke boldly that I was a new creation in Christ Jesus (2 Corinthians 5:17)! It doesn't matter how strong you are in the Lord, who you are, or your high-ranking status in this life—you will be tempted by the devil!

Jesus is the Son of God, and Satan even tempted Him (Matthew 4:1).

The Bible says that Satan comes to steal, kill and destroy (John 10:10). Accepting his advances will lead to the destruction of your plans and future! Accepting his lies and temptations will also lead to a divide of your precious relationship with God.

In order to defeat Satan and his devices, you must submit to God! Resist him and he will run from you (James 4:7). In Matthew chapter 4, Jesus had an answer for everything that Satan threw at Him. Jesus then told him to leave and Satan had no choice but to leave (Matthew 4:10-11). Jesus also reminded Satan of His identity—that He was God in the flesh (Matthew 1:23; Matthew 4:7). When I was getting tormented with those dreams, I had to remind Satan that I was a child of God, and I have the authority! I combated him by speaking Bible verses out loud against him (Ephesians 6:17). Beloved, when the enemy tries to tempt you and pull you back, remind him of your identity. Rebuke him, resist him, resist his devices, and speak against Him with Bible scriptures. Put on the full armor of God (Ephesians 6:13)! You are not fighting against human forces, but against spiritual forces that want to demolish your progress! When the devil reminds you of your past, remind him of his terrible future (Revelation 20:10). Remember your identity through Christ Jesus, your beautiful future (Jeremiah 29:11) and the blessings that God is giving you (Ecclesiastes 3:13).

Temptations can come in many ways. Whether it is that toxic relationship you're thinking about getting into or your old bad thoughts and habits. No matter what it is, don't give in. Stick close with your Father in Heaven; He will help you find an escape out of the temptation (1 Corinthians 10:13). Take some time and write down your temptations and ways that the enemy has been trying to pull you back. After you're done, put your hand on your list and say the daily prayer on the next page for God to destroy those plans in the name of Jesus.

Meditate

"Let not sin therefore reign in your mortal body, that ye should obey it in the lusts thereof."

Romans 6:12

"But the Lord is faithful, who shall stablish you, and keep you from all evil."

2 Thessalonians 3:3

"There hath no temptation taken you but such as is common to man: but God is faithful, who will not suffer you to be tempted above that ye are able; but will with the temptation also make a way to escape, that ye may be able to bear it."

1 Corinthians 10:13

"No evil weapon fashioned against thee shall prosper; and every tongue that shall rise against thee in judgment thou shalt condemn. This is the heritage of the servants of the LORD, and their righteousness is of me, saith the LORD."

Isaiah 54:17

Prayer

Father God, as my hand is upon this paper, I cancel every temptation that the enemy is using to destroy my life and plans in Jesus's name. I condemn every evil assignment made against my life in Jesus's name. I will not accept any of Satan's plans, temptation, or devices in the name of Jesus! No evil weapon fashioned against me shall prosper in Jesus's name! Lord, put on me the full offensive and defensive armor of God. Cancel every evil plan from Satan against my life, O Lord Jesus. We thank You, Lord Jesus. In Jesus's mighty name, I pray, amen.

Seek and You Shall Find

"But if from thence thou shalt seek the Lord thy God, thou shalt find him, if thou seek him with all thy heart and with all thy soul." Deuteronomy 4:29

Today's Scripture Reading:
2 Samuel 5:17-25; Psalm 63:1-8

Reading the Word of God, you will see that major events started with his people seeking and inquiring of Him. This was done by fasting, taking quiet time apart to spend with Him and through the most simple but powerful way—prayer. Why is seeking the Lord so important? Why is prayer important? Or is it just something that people say just to say? It wasn't until I started to spend time in prayer myself that I understood just how vital prayer really was.

Prayer gives us direct communication with the Father. Like picking up the phone to call your friend just to meet with them and talk with them, is just how it is with the Father. It is a form of therapy when you're stressed or down. He wants to know EVERYTHING. Through prayer, you give Him the opportunity to answer you, protect you, and lead you in the right direction. Sometimes we become frustrated when we are constantly praying to the Lord and we feel as if we are not getting an answer. But God is not a magician; He works on the best time—His time. He calls us to pray without ceasing (1 Thessalonians 5:17). He does this to make us continually SEEK Him actively. This builds the relationship between you and God and keeps that connection.

What if you asked the Lord for something, you finally got it, and afterward, you stopped praying to Him? What if you stopped asking Him what to do next? That set you up for failure because once you got what you "thought you needed," you were not able to maintain it because you didn't know what to do next. You had no one directing you. So, you received that gift without proper direction on how to maintain it. This is why we must seek the Lord in everything that we do.

You do not want to make the mistake of doing something outside of your specified season (Ecclesiastes 3:1) before God's appointed time. Doing something too early or moving in the wrong direction can delay your destiny. There was a time I really wanted to marry this man, a guy that I had been dating because I didn't want to fall into sexual sin. However, he was not the man that God appointed me to marry. If I had moved into marriage at that time, I would've missed my true husband, which would have led to the Lord rerouting my direction to my destiny, and Lord knows what else! It would have been a disaster that was not needed. But praise God, I sought His face every day on the matter until He gave me an answer....NO!

What if David went to battle without asking the Lord? Imagine what a problem that would have been. He could've lost everything, including the lives of the army following him, just because he would not inquire of His commander in chief. God gave him direct answers about what to do and how to move. He had to seek the Lord to get those directions.

You should seek the Lord just for the simple fact that being in His presence is so beautiful. There is so much love, comfort, and wisdom just waiting to fall on you when you are in the presence of God. Seek Him for his mysteries. Just like a friend, when you spend more time with them, you know more about them and they honor you by revealing their deepest parts of themselves. This is similar to God! There is so much that the Lord wants to share of Himself with you, but He needs that relationship with you. If you seek Him, you will truly find Him.

Pray when you are happy! Pray when you are down! Pray when you are confused or lost! Pray when you think that the Lord is not answering quickly enough! P.U.S.H. – Pray Until Something Happens!

There are several ways of praying. There is spiritual warfare prayer, closet prayer, and prayer where you can just pray in your car or the shower. It is important to partake in all. However, a simple prayer to the Lord, simply talking to Him like a loving father or dearest friend with respect, can go a long way. He hears you. What have you been continuously seeking the Lord about? What are some things on your heart that you simply want to share with the Lord? This can be anything. Write them down, then take them to your Father.

Meditate

"Pray without ceasing. In everything give thanks: for this is the will of God in Christ Jesus concerning you."

1 Thessalonians 5:17,18

"Seek the Lord and his strength, seek his face continually."

1 Chronicles 16:11

"And they that know thy name will put their trust in thee: for thou, LORD, hast not forsaken them that seek thee."

Psalm 9:10

"Oh God, thou art my God; early will I seek thee: my soul thirsteth for thee, my flesh longeth for thee in a dry and thirsty land, where no water is;"

Psalm 63:1

Prayer

Dear Lord,
I ask that You give me Your strength and grace to seek You. I ask, Father, that You give me a heart that delights in Your presence. Lord, help me to pray without ceasing and to spend every moment with You. Increase my prayer life, Lord. I thank You in advance. In Jesus's mighty name, amen.

_____

_____

_____

_____

_____

_____

_____

_____

_____

_____

_____

_____

_____

_____

_____

_____

_____

_____

_____

Keep Thy Lips

"O Set a watch, O Lord, before my mouth; keep the door of my lips." Psalm 141:3

Today's Scripture Reading:
Ecclesiastes 5:1-7; Ecclesiastes 10:11-14

When great things happen to us, we are often so excited to share it with anyone and everyone, including the people close to us, or sometimes to people we don't even know (or haven't talked to in a very long time). Wanting to share your accomplishments is not a bad thing! However, it is a bad thing to speak out of season. The word of God says in Ecclesiastes 3:7, "There is a time to be silent and a time to speak." It is good practice to go to the Lord to ask when it is the right time to share your achievements or even your hurts! We must have godly discernment in recognizing the time to speak. The reality of this life is that not everyone has your best interest at heart. In other cases, people may have your best interest at heart, but they themselves may not have a strong relationship with the Holy Spirit. Sharing sensitive information with these people may delay your progress because they may give you the wrong advice.

When I was getting married to my husband, we did not tell most of our friends or family. This is because we knew that the Lord was working in our lives a kingdom marriage. Since we only knew each other for a very short time before marriage, we knew that everyone's logical comments were going to be, "You don't know each other; it's not enough time." However, the Lord had revealed that my husband and I were destined to be married through prophecy. If we had told our friends who are not deep into the spiritual workings of God, we could have been led away with their "friendly" advice. Instead of seeking their counsel, the Holy Spirit led us to deep-rooted people of God, who fasted and ministered with us to consult the Lord. Now, at the time of writing this book, it has been a year and two months since we've been married. Constantly, the Lord continues to reveal to us the purpose of our marriage! Where would we have been if we had spoken too soon or to the wrong people? We, as children of God, need to learn when to keep our mouths closed!

James 1:19 says, "We should be slow to speak." We shouldn't speak too soon when a plan has not fully matured. We shouldn't be so quick to share things with people who may be enemies in disguise (Proverbs 21:23). We shouldn't speak important matters to people (even close companions) who the devil may use to derail us from what we are meant to accomplish. We should always be led by the Holy Spirit about when to speak, where to speak, and who we speak it to. Don't let anyone make you feel bad about not sharing something with them. As long as you are in the will of God about the issue, then you are just where you need to be. Explain to them your reasoning with love and without malice. If they truly have your best interest at heart, they will understand.

We might be quick to share certain things, but this is not how the Lord wants us to live. Your purpose and the things you are supposed to accomplish are very sacred and sensitive. Not everyone may understand what the Lord is doing in your life because it is YOUR life! Not their life. Be open to the Holy Spirit in letting Him lead you. What is the Lord telling you not to share? Has there been anything on your mind that you want to share, but your heart is not at ease about sharing? Meditate on these questions and ask your Father in heaven to reveal them to you. Write them down. Also, write down ways you can avoid talking about the subject when it is brought up. Practice speaking your answers out loud if you seem to be having trouble. Your kingdom destiny is before you.

Meditate

"Not that which goeth into the mouth defileth a man; but that which cometh out of the mouth, this defileth a man."

Matthew 15:11

"Whoso keepeth his mouth and his tongue keepeth his soul from troubles."

Proverbs 21:23

"Death and life are in the power of the tongue: and they that love it shall eat the fruit thereof."

Proverbs 18:21

"Let your speech be always with grace, seasoned with salt, that ye may know how ye ought to answer every man."

Colossians 4:6

Prayer

Dear Father, thank You for the blessings that You have placed upon my life. Please forgive me for any time that I have spoken out of season. Lord, I ask that You give me discernment to know when I should speak and keep quiet. Show me when and with whom I should share information. Lord, make me into a child of God who is slow to speak. Let me honor You with my lips. Lord, I ask that I receive honorable lips and not lips of a fool. I will not destroy or delay my destiny with my mouth, in Jesus's name! Holy Spirit, take control of my mouth. In Jesus's name, amen.

Declaration of Greatness

"Thou shalt also decree a thing, and it shall be established unto thee: and the light shall shine upon thy ways." Job 22:28

Today's Scripture Reading:
Matthew 21:18-22; Job 22:15-30

The tongue is a very powerful and dangerous tool. As we learned yesterday, not controlling our tongue can put us in detrimental situations. The word of God tells us that life and death are in the power of the tongue. (Proverbs 18:21). Are you speaking life to your situations, or are you speaking death? The situations that we should be speaking death to should be illness, lack, struggle, sin, disobedience, poverty and so forth! Through Jesus Christ, we have the authority to speak to any situation we are facing! This is only through Jesus Christ!

In the scripture, Jesus spoke to the fig tree that was not producing any fruit. When He commanded that no fruit should grow from then forward, it immediately withered away (Matthew 21:19)! He then told the disciples that if they had faith and didn't doubt, they would be able to do the same and even more (Matthew 21:21). With that authority given to us by Christ, we have His strength and power through Him to complete all things (Philippians 4:13)! As believers, we often become so down and heartbroken about the situations occurring in our lives that we forget the POWER that we have through Christ Jesus (2 Timothy 1:7). If our situations are not lining up with the promises that the Lord has blessed us with, we have the authority through His blood to declare His will over our lives! We don't have to stay in bondage! We don't have to stay in bondage to our sin; we don't have to stay in bondage to unhealthy addictions, we don't have to stay in bondage to poverty, illnesses, mental illness, etc. You must speak death to those things (just like Jesus did with the fig tree) and ask God to take those things away from you through faith in Christ!

The Bible says if we decree a thing (anything in the will of God), it shall be established unto us, and the light of God shall shine upon our ways (Job 22:28). Through Christ Jesus, we have the spiritual authority to declare greatness over our lives, and it shall come to pass. Here are a few examples of declarations you can speak over yourself:

In the name of Jesus, I decree and declare that I am healthy!

In the name of Jesus, I decree and declare that I am an obedient child of God!

In the name of Jesus, I decree and declare that I will succeed in my God-given purpose!

"So shall my word be that goeth forth out of my mouth: it shall not return unto me void, but it shall accomplish that which I please, and it shall prosper in the thing whereto I sent it." -Isaiah 55:11

The words that you speak through Christ will not be just empty words, but the words you speak shall be accomplished, and they shall prosper! The words that the Lord also have spoken over your life will be completed quickly and not prolonged in the name of Jesus (Ezekiel 12:28).

What other declarations has the Lord given you to speak over your life? Write them down. Speak them out loud every day! You can do this while you're walking, driving, showering or when you're before the presence of God. With faith in our Father Jesus, His strength and His power, you can speak to your life. By His will, you can speak to your situations, it will be established, and it will come to pass. (See Appendix C for more declarations).

Meditate

"So shall my word be that goeth forth out of my mouth: it shall not return unto me void, but it shall accomplish that which I please, and it shall prosper in the thing whereto I sent it."

Isaiah 55:11

"We having the same spirit of faith, according as it is written, I believed, and therefore have I spoken; we also believe, and therefore speak."

2 Corinthians 4:13

"Let no corrupt communication proceed out of your mouth, but that which is good to the use of edifying, that it may minister grace unto the hearers."

Ephesians 4:29

"For he spake, and it was done; he commanded, and it stood fast."

Psalm 33:9

Prayer

Dear Lord, I thank You for all the revelations that You have given me to speak over my life. Thank You for speaking greatness over my life. Thank You for using me for Your glory through the words You have spoken over my life. Please don't let any negative word spoken against my life from anyone, including myself, prosper. Let me always speak Your goodness over my life. I decree and declare that I will walk in faith in Jesus Christ. In Jesus's mighty name, amen.

_____

_____

_____

_____

_____

_____

_____

_____

_____

_____

_____

_____

_____

_____

_____

_____

_____

_____

_____

Come in With Thanks

"O give thanks unto the LORD, for he is good: for his mercy endureth forever." Psalm 107:1

Today's Scripture Reading:
Psalm 105; Psalm 106; Psalm 107; Luke 17:11-19

With the heavy responsibilities and demanding schedules we have, it can be difficult to think or even eat. There is no time to have for yourself just to enjoy life. Running from one meeting to the other, running to pick up your children from daycare. Working long hours, not even sleeping in the home that you are paying for. This life can be so intense and so demanding that you are often left feeling drained. You can become weary, leading you to start thinking about everything else you need to tackle. This then becomes a trail of stress, anxiety, and complaints.

We start to forget the blessings that we receive every day. Just getting up out of bed is a blessing! Instead of us thanking God for our job, we are at work, searching for a new job on our phones. Do you remember all those times that you spent crying for God to get you accepted into that school or to get that job? Now you want to fold because you've hit a few bumps in the road. Yes, this life is hectic, and our responsibilities increase every moment, but it's not going to help us if we continue meditating on the negative. IN ALL THINGS, the Lord says we should give thanks for this is His will concerning us (1 Thessalonians 5:18). That is a commandment! When we keep a mind of thanks, it starts to reflect in our attitudes and our lives. This also makes the Lord happy because it shows that we appreciate what He gives us, and no matter the difficulties, we are ready to receive more blessings. This will open the gates of stored up blessings for your life to receive what the Father has been keeping for you.

How can He give you more when you are complaining so much about what you have? It shows from your attitude and behavior that you cannot handle the present blessings, but you want God to give you more. How would you feel if we kept giving emotionally, spiritually and or tangibly to someone, and they never said thank you? This would hurt us, so imagine how God feels...

Having a mindset of thanksgiving leads to having a heart of praise. This paves the way for the action of worship—forming that powerful relationship with Him in spirit and in truth (John 4:24). We need to take time and think about everything the Lord has done for us, where He brought us from, where He is taking us. This is illustrated in chapters 105, 106, and 107 of the book of Psalms, where all of God's goodness and miracles were demonstrated toward His people.

When we come before the Lord in prayer, before asking Him for anything, let us give thanks for all that He has provided. When God honors us and answers our prayers, we should not be like the nine lepers that did not come back to give God gratitude (Luke 17:17-18). Let us always come into His presence with thanksgiving.

Every time you read the Word of God, I challenge you to point out scriptures that discuss giving thanks. Even Kings gave thanks unto our Lord! So, King or Queen, what are you thankful for? What has the Lord done for you? What cries unto the Lord did He answer? Write them here as a reminder that God has so much more for you, especially when you give Him thanks.

Meditate

"Enter into his gates with thanksgiving, and into his courts with praise: be thankful unto him, and bless his name."

Colossians 4:2

"In every thing give thanks: for this is the will of God in Christ Jesus concerning you."

1 Thessalonians 5:18

"O give thanks unto the LORD; call upon his name: make known his deeds among the people."

Psalm 105:1

Prayer

Dear Lord, thank You for everything that You have done in my life. Thank You for where You brought me from and where You are taking me. Forgive me for any time that I have complained and did not appreciate You. Lord, give me a heart of thanksgiving so that I can praise and worship You in a way that is pleasing to You. Let me meditate on Your goodness and mercy. In Jesus's name I pray, amen.

_____

_____

_____

_____

_____

_____

_____

_____

_____

_____

_____

_____

_____

_____

_____

_____

_____

_____

_____

_____

_____

Purity

"Blessed are the pure in heart: for they shall see God." Matthew 5:8

Today's Scripture Reading:
Matthew 5:1-10

When people hear the word "purity," what may come to mind is simply keeping themselves before marriage or abstaining from fornication (both of which are true). However, these are not the only definitions of purity when it comes to understanding God and His will for your life.

God's will for our lives calls for us to have a pure heart. "I think I have a pure heart. I'm a nice person. I give to the poor. I do nice things for people." Being a nice person and doing nice things does not mean you have a pure heart. The Bible says that all have sinned and come short of the glory of God (Romans 3:23). The Bible also says, "The heart is deceitful above all things and desperately wicked (Jeremiah 17:9)." That means that your natural heart is wicked and deceitful. None of us are perfect nor have a good heart. We do things for self-gain, and none of us are righteous (Romans 3:10). So how can we obtain a pure heart for God's standard? Psalms 119:9 says, "Wherewithal shall a young man cleanse his way? By taking heed thereto according to thy word." In order to cleanse your way and your heart, you must follow the Lord and His commandments, yielding and submitting to the word of God. You must obey Him and be not just a hearer of His word, but a doer (James 1:22). "I am the Almighty God; walk before me and be thou perfect (Genesis 17:1)." Walking before the Lord and following His instructions in the Bible and what He speaks for you to do will make you perfect! When you follow Him, He will perfect you and purify you.

When you walk in the way of the Lord, you will go in His perfect path for your life. He will lead you with His perfection with the Holy Spirit, checking your heart and motives in every way. When the Lord sees that you are walking in His will and His perfection, He will excel you. When you're moving in His will, you will have a pure heart and you will see God (Matthew 5:8). When you have a pure heart, you will not only see God at the end of your life, but also throughout your journey of life.

Would you like to see the face of God in your life? In order for you to see God, you must be pure in heart, and to obtain purity, you must walk in the way of the Lord. Write down areas where you are struggling to follow God and His commandments. Write down areas where it is difficult for you to obey His voice and His will for your life. Ask the Lord to help you and let Him give you a pure heart in all things that you do.

Meditate

"Blessed are the undefiled in the way, who walk in the law of the Lord."

Psalm 119:1

"Thy word is very pure: therefore thy servant loveth it."

Psalm 119:140

"Do good, O Lord, unto those that be good, and to them that are upright in their hearts."

Psalm 125:4

"A new heart also will I give you, and a new spirit will I put within you: and I will take away the stony heart out of your flesh, and I will give you and heart of flesh."

Ezekiel 36:26

Prayer

Dear Lord, thank You for revealing to me where I fall short of Your Glory. Lord, please cleanse my way and help me to follow You. Lord, lead me to obey You. Create in me a pure heart so that I may see You throughout my life and at the end of my journey. Purify my way and my motives. Perfect me in Your will, O Lord. I ask this of You in Jesus's name, amen.

_____

_____

_____

_____

_____

_____

_____

_____

_____

_____

_____

_____

_____

_____

_____

_____

_____

_____

_____

_____

_____

_____

_____

_____

_____

_____

_____

_____

_____

_____

_____

_____

_____

_____

_____

_____

_____

_____

_____

_____

Heavenly Bank Account?

"Honour the Lord with thy substance, and with the firstfruits of all thine increase:" Proverbs 3:9

Today's Scripture Reading:
Malachi 3:6-18

Do you ever wonder where all your tithes and offering go? This is a question that I hear from many believers. They often wonder if the money they've worked hard for is going toward the church's needs or the pastor's new shoes. This thought can come from a place of genuine curiosity, or it can be just another reason to withhold what rightfully belongs to God.

Giving your tithes is one of the most important things that you can do for yourself in this life. Giving your tithes and offering is a sign of respect unto the Lord. Refusing to give your tithes and offering for any reason is disobedience unto the Lord that won't go unpunished (Malachi 3:9). Every good gift comes from the Father of lights (God) (James 1:17). He is the One that blesses you with increase (1 Corinthians 3:6).

Can a man rob God? God is not mocked. If there is one thing I've learned, it's that giving of tithes can save your life. I have encountered many people's testimonies that either they or their children were saved from death because they gave tithes. This was revealed unto them. Even with my own testimony, I have not lacked because I have tested God and faithfully given my tithes and offering. When you give your tithes, God says that He will rebuke the destroyer for you. He will cast down the enemy from destroying your growth in business, finances and any other area in your life due to your obedience (Malachi 3:11). The first-fruits, or the 10 percent, belong to God. Out of a dollar, that is 10 cents, out of 20, that is two dollars (Leviticus 27:30; Proverbs 3:9); a small sacrifice in exchange for your honor to God.

Do you ever wonder why certain things aren't going well in your life or why your plans keep failing? Or It seems like your finances continue to be drained, either on car problems, business ventures that did not go through, etc.? When was the last time you gave your tithes, love? If you don't give God your tithes and offering, the enemy will always use this against you to destroy all that you are trying to build! The Lord says to test Him! He says give what belongs to Him, and He will open the windows of heaven and pour upon you blessings that are so much you won't even have room to hold all of it (Malachi 3:10)! These are God's words, not mine! God honors those who obey Him!

It is not your business to know what the pastor or the church is doing with the money you give to God. However, it is your business to give unto God so His storage houses can be filled, and all those who need assistance can receive through Him (Malachi 3:10). If those in the church's higher positions are misusing God's fruits, then that curse will be left on their heads. YOU are responsible for your part; vengeance belongs to God (Romans 12:19).

Giving that which you think is small but belongs to God will reap for you scores of blessings in your heavenly bank account. Test the Lord; make a declaration to give back what belongs to Him. He wants every part of you, including your finances, because where your treasure is, that is where your heart is also (Matthew 6:21). Where is your heart? Is it with our Father, or with your material gains on this earth that will one day perish (Matthew 6:19)? Jot down reasons why you struggle with paying your tithes and offering. Write down, "Lord, I will try you according to your word, Malachi 3:10." Write down areas where you would like the Lord to bless you. According to His perfect will for your life, He will bless you (Matthew 7:11).

Meditate

"Honour the Lord with thy substance, and with the firstfruits of all thine increase: So shall thy barns be filled with plenty, and thy presses shall burst out with new wine."

Proverbs 3:9,10

"But lay up for yourselves treasures in heaven, where neither moth nor rust doth corrupt, and where thieves do not break through nor steal: For where your treasure is, there will your heart be also."

Matthew 6:20,21

"I fast twice in the week, I give tithes of all that I possess."

Luke 18:12

"And blessed be the most high God, which hath delivered thine enemies into thy hand. And he gave him tithes of all."

Genesis 14:20

Prayer

Dear Lord, thank You for revealing to me my need to give tithes and offering. Reveal and lead me to where I should give Your tithes and offering. Please forgive me for all the times that I have robbed You. As I test You, O Lord, please restore all that was taken from me and replenish my life with multitudes of Your blessings. Open Your windows of blessings over my life. Give me the heart to honor and respect You. Give me the heart to obey You. I seal these words in the blood of Jesus. In Jesus's mighty name, amen.

_____

_____

_____

_____

_____

_____

_____

_____

_____

_____

_____

_____

_____

_____

_____

_____

_____

_____

_____

_____

_____

A Humble Heart

"But he giveth more grace. Wherefore he saith, God resisteth the proud, but giveth grace unto the humble." James 4:6

Today's Scripture Reading:
Isaiah 14:12-15; Ezekiel 28:12-18; Philippians 2:5-8

Humility is a key to success and a key to God's heart. When you have a humble heart, you are open to following the instructions of the Lord, and He can use you. James 4:10 says, "Humble yourselves in the sight of the Lord, and he shall lift you up." When you come with respect and honor before the Father, He will honor you (Luke 14:10). God disregards a haughty and prideful heart, and this is usually the downfall of people who reach high levels in their careers. Once people start to receive all the financial blessings and promotions and are doing exceptionally well in their business and life in general, they start feeling like they have it made. They think that they are on top of the world (James 4:14-16). However, the Lord said that we should not trust in riches (Psalm 62:10, Proverbs 11:28).

Due to our sinful nature, it is very easy to cross that line and become prideful. The Lord hates pride and being prideful will lead to your destruction (Proverbs 6:16-17, Proverbs 16:18). Therefore, it is extremely important for you to check your own life every day. Check your attitude. Check how you treat others. Evaluate your actions and your inner thoughts. Ask the Lord to search you and to take out anything within you that He does not like (Psalm 139:23-24). Ask the Lord to cleanse your heart daily. If you struggle with being humble, there is a pruning process that God must do within you. Although it may hurt, the Lord will greatly bless you. Lucifer (Satan) was an angel whom God loved dearly. God anointed him and blessed him with beautiful jewels and more (Ezekiel 28:13). His heart became so lifted up and prideful because of his beauty that he wanted to overthrow the very God who created him (Ezekiel 28:17, Isaiah 14:13-15)! Due to Satan's pride, the Lord cast him out of heaven, and he lost the high and anointed position that the Lord gave him. He then became the devil. You can lose EVERYTHING because of pride.

However, let us model Jesus. Although He is the Son of God, he came to earth in the flesh and humbled himself as a servant to complete the work of God (Philippians 2:7-8). His humility allowed Him to obey God, and today He sits on the right hand of the power of God (Luke 22:69).

Humility is not just shown from the outward appearance, but it comes from your heart. You need God to renew you so that it becomes your lifestyle, a genuine part of you. God wants to bless us, but He cannot do it with sin in our hearts that leads to destruction. Let God take you higher by you becoming lowly. Try Him and let humility and blessings join hands in your life.

"By humility and the fear of the Lord are riches, and honour, and life." - Proverbs 22:4

Search yourself and jot down areas in your life where you need humility. Be honest! You might find these areas difficult in days to come, but return here to write them down. Let the Lord heal you and renew you in these areas so that you may complete His blessed will for your life.

Meditate

"Put on therefore, as the elect of God, holy and beloved, bowels of mercies, kindness, humbleness of mind, meekness, longsuffering;"

Colossians 3:12

"If my people, which are called by my name, shall humble themselves, and pray, and seek my face, and turn from their wicked ways; then will I hear from heaven, and will forgive their sin, and will heal their land."

2 Chronicles 7:14

"For whosoever exalteth himself shall be abased; and he that humbleth himself shall be exalted."

Luke 14:11

"When pride cometh, then cometh shame: but with the lowly is wisdom."

Proverbs 11:2

Prayer

Father, I ask You to renew in me a new heart. Dear Lord, where there is pride in my life, I ask that You replace it with humility. Lord, let my heart please You from here on out. Lord, suppress my flesh. As I become successful, Lord, continue to remove pride from my heart, life, and spirit. Let me have a humble heart before You and let my life reflect humility. Thank You in advance. In Jesus's mighty name, amen.

_____

_____

_____

_____

_____

_____

_____

_____

_____

_____

_____

_____

_____

_____

_____

_____

_____

_____

_____

_____

Take Wise Counsel

"Where no counsel is, the people fall: but in the multitude of counsellors there is safety." Proverbs 11:14

Today's Scripture Reading:
1 Kings 22:1-38

When you read and study the word of God, you will most likely see that many of the Kings always had counselors. These counselors were either wise men or prophets who communed with God.

In the scripture reading, the Bible talked about the evil King Ahab and how his lack of receiving Godly counsel led to his death. When King Jehoshaphat and King Ahab were discussing going to war, King Jehoshaphat wanted to receive counsel from the Lord. When a prophet of God (Micaiah) came to give them counsel, Ahab rejected it because it was not the answer he wanted to hear. He wanted to do what he wanted to do. To his dismay, King Ahab did not know that the other prophets were giving him false advice and false assurances to make war. These false prophets were all led by a lying spirit (1 Kings 22:22-23). Taking this unwise counsel, King Ahab was led to his death (1 Kings 22:37-38).

As a believer who is moving toward your Godly destiny, it is important to keep friends in your corner who are led by the Holy Spirit. The Bible tells us that bad company corrupts good character (1 Corinthians 15:33). You become like those who you spend most of your time around. If they have bad characteristics, those will rub off on you. If the people around you do not have the fear (reverence) for God, they can easily be used by the enemy to derail you from your Godly purpose. They can give you bad advice and even have you walking against God. In the scripture reading, we see that if it were not for the mercy of God, King Jehoshaphat would have lost his life by listening to the destructive plans of King Ahab (1 King 22:30-33)!

If you want your life to flourish, it is important to seek God in all things. Through the discretion of the Holy Spirit, you will be directed to Godly and wise counselors in your life, such as parents, advisors, friends, teachers, pastors, etc. Do not disregard the truth for your own comfort and lean not on your own understanding (Proverbs 3:5). The Lord loves you, so He will always correct you when you're wrong or going in the wrong direction (Proverbs 3:12). Do not let pride get in the way of following God-given and wise advice. It might just cost you your future...

Who are you keeping in your circle? Do those people tell you the truth? Or do they just tell you what you want to hear? Do you choose to ignore counsel just because it's not pleasing to you? Remember that God corrects you because He wants you to walk in His purpose. What has God been giving you counsel about? Who has He been using to speak to you? Are the people around you close to God, or do you feel they might be leading you away? Why is it difficult for you to accept wise and Godly counsel? Truly search yourself with the Holy Spirit and write down your answers.

Meditate

"Poverty and shame shall be to him that refuseth instruction: but he that regardeth reproof shall be honoured."

Proverbs 13:18

"Blessed is the man that walketh not in the counsel of the ungodly, nor standeth in the way of sinners, nor sitteth in the seat of the scornful;"

Psalm 1:1

"For the commandment is a lamp; and the law is light; and reproofs of instruction are the way of life."

Proverbs 6:23

"Behold, happy is the man whom God correcteth: therefore despise not thou the chastening of the Almighty."

Job 5:17

Prayer

Dear Father, I thank You for being the Lord of my life. Lord, I thank You for always covering my steps and bringing me this far in my life. Dear Lord, please lead me in the way of wise counsel. Lord, help me always to accept wise and Godly advice no matter how my flesh feels. Please remove from my life the friends and associates who are leading me away from You. Replace them with people who will lead me to do Your will. Dear Jesus, let Your Holy Spirit help me to obey. In Jesus's mighty name, amen.

_____

_____

_____

_____

_____

_____

_____

_____

_____

_____

_____

_____

_____

_____

_____

_____

_____

_____

_____

_____

Unshakeable Faith

"But without faith it is impossible to please him: for he that cometh to God must believe that he is, and that he is a rewarder of them that diligently seek him." Hebrews 11:6

Today's Scripture Reading:
Hebrews 11; Hebrews 12:1,2

One day when I was in college, I was in my dorm room, crying my eyes out. There was so much going on in my life. My family lost our home to foreclosure, leading to our eviction. I had to help support my family emotionally and financially. I also had to support myself in the midst of it all. My grades were dropping, and I couldn't understand anything I was learning. I was so alone. "God, this is not what you promised me," is what I spoke in sadness. That's when I heard the Lord say, "Do you trust me?" I jumped up! His voice sounded like a million deep waters flowing and shaking. His voice shook me! This wasn't in my mind; it was his actual voice! This was the same way He spoke to His people in times of old! I couldn't believe I heard the voice of my God so powerfully!

I verbally spoke and said, "Yes, Lord. Of course, I trust you." It was because of that experience that no matter what, I never gave up. No matter what pain, hurt, and failures I experienced, I kept pushing. I wouldn't be where I am if it weren't for Him!

Without faith, you cannot serve God (Hebrews 11:6). Without faith, you cannot walk in the destiny that God has designed for you. It is by the grace of God through faith that we are saved from all of our life's struggles until the day the Lord brings us home to Himself (Ephesians 2:8). If our Father can provide for the birds in the air and the flowers in the field, what more about us (Matthew 6:26-30)?

Throughout the Bible, we can see how the Lord came through for His people. He parted the Red Sea so the Hebrews could escape the hands of the Egyptians (Hebrews 11:29). He promised and gave Sara a child, even though she was beyond the age of giving birth (Hebrews 11:11-12). The Lord revealed to Noah that He was bringing a great flood upon the earth. By faith, Noah obeyed and built the ark, which the Lord used to save his entire family (Hebrews 11:7). Anyone who commits to a deep relationship with God, He makes them victorious (Romans 8:37). This is the God who saved His people and brought the promises to His children to pass. This same God, who is the same yesterday, today, and forever (Hebrews 13:8), completed powerful deeds! He did great things through faith for all these people, so what makes you think that He cannot do it for you? This and so much more He has done! Beloved, this is the same God that you serve! So much more He is going to do through you.

Do not be afraid of the great places the Lord is going to take you. Do not be afraid of your potential because greater is Christ that is in you than the evil that is in the world (1 John 4:4). Do not be afraid to fall or fail because the good man falls several times and still gets up (Proverbs 24:16). You must have UNSHAKEABLE faith! Nothing should move your faith, knowing that the God you serve is a loving God, a dream giver, a life accomplisher, a God of action! You must reassure yourself in the Word of God. Notice I said IN and not WITH. Because when you are IN the Word, you and the Lord become one, and you allow Him to move profoundly (John 1:1).

Sometimes you may see others accomplishing the same goals that you are trying to accomplish. As much as you are happy for them, it may still hurt because you feel that you have been dealt the wrong hand in life. You feel that you have had many setbacks, many disappointments. Beloved, do not be discouraged (Isaiah 41:10)! The Lord has never forgotten you. He is with you, paving the way. There are just a few areas where He needs to build you so you can be the best. He is building a solid foundation within you, so if anything comes to try and shake you, you're going to stand tall (Ephesians 6:13). You are a child of God, full of faith. Put on your Christ attire and excel!

As I reflect on my life and all that the Lord has brought me through, I think, where would I have been if my faith was shortened? *The Lord, your God, wants you to exemplify unshakeable faith! If faith the size of a mustard seed can move mountains, where would faith that is unmeasurable take you (Matthew 17:20)? Faith that cannot be broken? Declare today that you will have unshakeable faith! How do you want faith to change your life? How do you want faith to change your relationship with Christ? What areas in your life need more faith? Write them down. The Lord is asking you today, do you trust Him? No matter the current situation in your life, always walk by faith in your God (2 Corinthians 5:7).*

Meditate

"So then faith cometh by hearing, and hearing by the word of God."

Romans 10:17

"I have fought a good fight, I have finished my course, I have kept the faith:"

2 Timothy 4:7

"Now the just shall live by faith: but if any man draw back, my soul shall have no pleasure in him."

Hebrews 10:38

"Now faith is the substance of things hoped for, the evidence of things not seen."

Hebrews 11:1

Prayer

Dear Father, thank you for saving me by grace through faith. Lord Jesus, I ask today that You renew my faith. Father, I ask that You give me unshakeable faith. Lord Jesus, I ask that You please give me an unmeasurable amount of faith. Give me faith in abundance; let my cup of faith run over. Help me remember where You brought me from, and give me hope of where You are taking me. Lord, let my trust in You be unshakeable. Even when the path seems dark, Lord, let Your light shine upon me. I thank You for everything. In Jesus's mighty name, amen.

_____

_____

_____

_____

_____

_____

_____

_____

_____

_____

_____

_____

_____

_____

_____

_____

_____

_____

_____

_____

_____

_____

Appendix A:
Inviting Christ as Your Personal Savior

If you haven't accepted Christ as your Savior and you want to invite Him into your life, here is a prayer that you can say:

My Lord, my God. Father, I know that I am a sinner who needs your forgiveness. I confess every sin I have done, those known and unknown, unto you. I believe that Jesus Christ died on the cross for me and rose again. I believe that He shed His precious and innocent blood for me. Dear Lord, I ask that you cleanse me with the blood of Jesus Christ. Dear Lord, I want to turn away from my sins and follow you. I invite Christ to come into my heart to become my personal Savior. In Jesus's precious name, amen.

When you pray this prayer, pray it earnestly and genuinely. Accepting Christ as your personal Savior means that you are inviting Him into your life. You are inviting Him to have a personal relationship with you, teach you, comfort you, and correct you. You should say this prayer only if you earnestly believe that Christ died on the Cross for your sins so you can be free from sin and death (spiritual death; Hell).

"If we confess our sins, he is faithful and just to forgive us our sins, and to cleanse us from all unrighteousness." 1 John 1:9

"For God so loved the world, that he gave his only begotten Son, that whosoever believeth in him should not perish, but have everlasting life." John 3:16

"That if thou shalt confess with thy mouth the Lord Jesus, and shalt believe in thine heart that God hath raised him from the dead, thou shalt be saved." Romans 10:9

If you want a fulfilling life with Christ and to be with Him in Heaven, here are the steps:

Admit to God that you are a sinner in need of Him as your Savior (Romans 3:10).

Repent to God, tell Him you are sorry for every sin you have committed, and you are willing to turn away from your sins.

Trust and believe in Jesus Christ, that He came to die for you on the cross, and He rose from the dead.

Now, invite Him into your heart with the above prayer to make Him your personal Savior.

After you say this prayer, you are now SAVED! The Kingdom of Heaven is rejoicing for you!

"Likewise, I say to you, there is joy in the presence of the angels of God over one sinner who repents." Luke 15:10

Now that you have trusted Christ, be sure to:

Read the Word of God every day (The Bible). Stay connected with Christ and His Holy Spirit that lives within you.

Pray each day to your Father in Heaven.

Get baptized. Attend a church that is filled with truth and power in the Holy Spirit! May the Bible be the book that they preach from, and Christ be the Savior and whom they follow. Fellowship with other believers and serve with other believers.

Make sure to tell others about Christ and all the amazing things He has done for you.

Send any questions you may have about God and your new Christian walk to heisdivinepub@gmail.com.

Follow @he_is_divine3 on Instagram for Christ-inspired content!

Appendix B:
Fasting 101

"But seek ye first the kingdom of God, and his righteousness; and all these things shall be added unto you."

-Matthew 6:33

"For the kingdom of God is not meat and drink; but righteousness, and peace, and joy in the Holy Ghost."

-Romans 14:17

"For the kingdom of God is not in word, but in power."

-1 Corinthians 4:20

"Is not this the fast that I have chosen? to loose the bands of wickedness, to undo the heavy burdens, and to let the oppressed go free, and that ye break every yoke?"

-Isaiah 58:6

Fasting is when you seek God on an issue and are pleading for the Lord to move on your behalf. You could also be seeking God to give you direction, or you could be fasting just to spend time with the Lord. The key here is SEEKING GOD. Whatever the reason you are fasting, you should always remember that God, His will, and His righteousness are the first and most important results, and all else that is good is added from His goodness (Matthew 6:33).

There are many Bible events where the people fasted for God's presence and God's intervention. One example is when Queen Esther and all the Jews fasted for three days when there was an order for all the Jews to be killed (Esther 4:6-17).

Daniel is also another notable person who fasted (Daniel 1:12; Daniel 10:2,3). In the flesh, our Savior, Jesus, also fasted for 40 days and 40 nights (Matthew 4:1,2).

There are different types and lengths of fasts that you can do according to what God is placing on your heart. There are fasts where some may do without consuming food for a certain number of hours or days. Example:

3-day fast with no food
3-day fast with no food for 6-12 hours
7-day fast for 6 hours with no food
7-day fast of just water, fruit and/or vegetables
5-day fast of skipping dinner
4-day fast from 6 am-12 pm with no food

Some people may do without certain types of food such as dairy, meat, processed foods, sugars and caffeine. There are some fasts where you would eat no food besides eating fruit and drinking water. I would not recommend fasting without water unless you are really, really seasoned in the Lord. Move at the pace of what you can handle and where God leads, not just because others are doing it! Fasting is personal and it is what the Lord is leading you to do. When you are fasting, you reject your fleshly desires and distractions to be very close to your Father. You are sacrificing your flesh to hear Him more clearly and to be more connected with Him in spirit. So, during your fast, you should spend most of your time with God in praying and reading His word. You should limit your time from people and things that distract your attention from hearing the voice of God.

Here are ways to take advantage of your time fasting before the Lord:

Making a list of what you're seeking God for
Writing revelations in your Journal
Journaling to God
Reading, studying and meditating on the Word of God
Praying
Worshiping the Lord
Listening to worship music (I found that this gave me strength when I was weak from not eating or tempted to eat)
Meditating on what the Lord is telling you
Watching faith-based preaching, messages, testimonies or videos as the Lord leads.

Here are the Don'ts of fasting:

Spending too much time with people; going out with friends and family
Spending time on social media
Telling people that you are fasting (Matthew 6:18)
Watching tv or listening to music that is not glorifying God
Participating in actions that are sinful or don't glorify God
Fasting when pregnant!

I recommend staying away from places that have food. If you're at a place for work or school where it is unavoidable, simply tell people that you really don't feel like eating and you'll eat later. Make sure that you still look nice and presentable! Just because you're fasting doesn't mean you have to look unkempt; you can still look clean and nice (Matthew 6:16-18). No one should know that you are fasting unless you've planned to fast with someone, and you are all on the same page about why you are fasting. But people who are not fasting with you should not know. For what you do in private, the Lord will reward you openly (Matthew 6:6).

Being around people can cause distractions and they might not be talking about things that are glorying God. So to not allow others to cloud hearing God's voice, it's best to limit contact with people while you're fasting. The whole point of your fast is to be closer to God, right? So, use this time wisely and to your advantage. Social media should be an absolute don't to fasting because there are so many images and messages that pop up that you cannot control. You don't want anything to taint your mind when you are before the presence of God.

The presence of God moving closer in your life should be the most important goal! Shaking the sin of your fleshly nature to seek Christ is the most fulfilling! As you become closer to God, He will lead you and instruct you on the fast you should take. If you are a beginner, you can start out with three days reserving at least four hours before the Lord with no food and soaking in the presence of God. If you cannot fast due to health reasons, talk with the Lord about an alternative. It could be you setting aside certain time away from the phone, distractions, tv, etc. to be away in His presence. Remember, whether you eat or drink, or neither eat nor drink, do it all for the Glory of God (1 Corinthians 10:31).

"[6] Is not this the fast that I have chosen? to loose the bands of wickedness, to undo the heavy burdens, and to let the oppressed go free, and that ye break every yoke? [7] Is it not to deal thy bread to the hungry, and that thou bring the poor that are cast out to thy house? when thou seest the naked, that thou cover him; and that thou hide not thyself from thine own flesh? [8] Then shall thy light break forth as the morning, and thine health shall spring forth speedily: and thy righteousness shall go before thee; the glory of the LORD shall be thy reward. [9] Then shalt thou call, and the LORD shall answer; thou shalt cry, and he shall say, Here I am. If thou take away from the midst of thee the yoke, the putting forth of the finger, and speaking vanity; [10] And if thou draw out thy soul to the hungry, and satisfy the afflicted soul; then shall thy light rise in obscurity, and thy darkness be as the noon day: [11] And the LORD shall guide thee continually, and satisfy thy soul in drought, and make fat thy bones: and thou shalt be like a watered garden, and like a spring of water, whose waters fail not."

Isaiah 58:6-11

Appendix C:
Declarations

Here are a few examples of declaration statements that you can say over yourself each day!

In the name of Jesus, I decree and declare that:

My soul is vibrant
I am victorious
I have all that I need
I am knowledgeable
I am full of wisdom
I am debt-free
I am strong
My family will make heaven
I am talented
I have a happy home
My children are blessed
My spouse is faithful
I am equipped
I will never lack
I am anointed
I am creative
I am beautiful
I am crowned with favor
I am approved
I am accepted
I am valuable
I am the head
I am a leader
I am wise

I am confident
I am royalty
I am prosperous
I am joyful
I am wonderful
My name is in the Book of Life

Remember that you can always add more declarations as the Lord places them on your heart. You can declare for your family; you can even declare for the world to make godly changes.

Sometimes we may be tempted to speak negatively against ourselves or our family when difficult situations arise. However, this is not what God wants us to do. He wants us to speak life into ourselves and the people who are dear in our lives. Declare greatness each and every day!

Appendix D:
Tithing

Tithing is taking out 10 percent that **belongs** to God from what you've earned or received.

Offering is what you **choose** to give to God.

When I tithe, I usually calculate it from my gross income (before taxes and everything else is taken out) because that is the amount that I actually earned and worked for. I recommend taking out your tithes and offering before paying bills or taking out any other money that needs to be spent. This will help to remind you always to put God first. I also take out tithes if someone has given me money. For example, if someone gave me $20, I would always take $2 out. I respect the Lord and want to honor Him in all ways the best that I can, even in the things that are considered little. What you think is little, God thinks of very highly.

Examples:
Your gross income:
$2,000------ You give $200 in tithes
$657.00-----You give $65.70 in tithes
$350,023------You give $35,002.30 in tithes
The decimal is always moved 1 place to the left.
If using a calculator multiply the gross income by 0.10:
879.23 (gross income) X 0.10= $87.92 tithes

You try:
A) 98.76
B) $70,098
C) $5,466
D) $30.45

E) $46,758,909

F) $3.00

Answer key on next page

ANSWER KEY:
A) *$9.88*
B) *$7,009.80*
C) *$546.60*
D) *$3.05*
E) *$4,675,890.90*
F) *$0.30*

Keep in Touch!

Send us testimonies, prayers, and questions.

He Is Divine Publications:

Instagram:
@he_is_divine3

Email:
heisdivinepub@gmail.com

Blessing JK Monday:
Instagram: @Sujahlov3

Made in the USA
Monee, IL
20 December 2020